BIBLICAL
PSYCHOLOGY

CHRIST-CENTERED SOLUTIONS
FOR DAILY PROBLEMS

BIBLICAL PSYCHOLOGY

OSWALD CHAMBERS

AUTHOR OF **MY UTMOST FOR HIS HIGHEST**

DISCOVERY HOUSE
PUBLISHERS®

Biblical Psychology

© 1962 Oswald Chambers Publications Association Limited

This edition © 1995 Oswald Chambers Publications Association Limited

Discovery House Publishers is affiliated with RBC Ministries, Grand Rapids, Michigan.

Requests for permission to quote from this book should be directed to: Permissions Department, Discovery House Publishers, P.O. Box 3566, Grand Rapids, MI 49501, or contact us by e-mail at permissionsdept@dhp.org

Library of Congress Cataloging-in-Publication Data
Chambers, Oswald, 1874-1917.
Biblical psychology: Christ-centered solutions for daily problems / by Oswald Chambers.
    p. cm.
Includes index.

ISBN 0-929239-60-1

1. Bible—Psychology. 2. Christian life—Biblical teaching. 3. Christianity—Psychology. 4. Man (Christian theology). I. Title.
BS645.C45   1995   233—dc20   95-32209
                                            CIP

Printed in the United States of America
Tenth printing in 2011

CONTENTS

PUBLISHER'S FOREWORD

Oswald Chambers immersed himself in the study of the inner man as revealed through the pages of Scripture. In addition, he was a discerning observer of the human condition explored in the writings of the great philosophers, theologians, novelists, poets, and playwrights. The books on his shelves ranged from Plato and Augustine to Victor Hugo and Henrik Ibsen.

Out of Chambers' study, he developed a series of lectures he called "Biblical Psychology"—the study of man from the Bible's point of view. These lectures constitute the core of Chambers' theology and psychology of man. They are keenly insightful and thoroughly biblical. Chambers states in the text, "It is these fundamental theological facts which must safeguard our psychological studies."

Biblical Psychology was compiled from Mrs. Chambers' verbatim notes of the lectures given at the Bible Training College,

London, during 1911. The book was first published in 1912, and revised editions have been issued through the years.

In these studies we get a revealing picture of Oswald Chambers the teacher and theologian. He looks at the psychology of our inner life and how we relate to ourselves, to others, and to God. He explores the moral dilemmas and emotional complexities believers face as they try to reconcile their faith with a world full of fear, anger, shame, and selfishness; and he offers scriptural answers for these struggles.

The publisher is honored to present this new updated edition of *Biblical Psychology* to the Christian world. The book's themes and approach show Chambers at his most profound, yet the insights are so biblical and simple that any student of the Word can be nourished by its pages. Here Chambers truly feeds the soul with the Word of God.

The Publisher

1

MAN: HIS CREATION, CALLING, AND COMMUNION[1]

1. **Conditions Before Man's Creation—Genesis 1:1**
   (a) Celestial Creations—Job 38:4–7
   (b) Celestial Catastrophe—Isaiah 14:12; Luke 10:18
   (c) Celestial Condemnation—John 8:44; Jude 6
2. **Conditions Leading to Man's Creation—Nehemiah 9:6**
   (a) Terrestrial Chaos—Genesis 1:2
   (b) Terrestrial Creations—Genesis 1:2–25
   (c) Terrestrial Cosmos—Genesis 1:4, 10, 12, 18, 21, 25, 31

---

1. Although the passages quoted appear as texts, they are really portions of connected revelation.

3. Climax of Creation—Genesis 1:26–27
   (a) The Son of God—Genesis 1:27; Luke 3:38
   (b) The Six Days' Work—Genesis 1:28–31
   (c) The Sabbath Rest—Genesis 2:1–3

1. Conditions Before Man's Creation

In the beginning God created the heavens and the earth. The earth was without form, and void; and darkness was on the face of the deep; and the Spirit of God was hovering over the face of the waters. (Genesis 1:1–2)

Between verses 1 and 2 of the first chapter of Genesis, there is a great hiatus. Verse 1 refers to an order of things before the reconstruction referred to in 2.

(a) Celestial Creations

We mean by celestial creations, the creations that were before human beings and the system of things as we understand them. These celestial creations belong to a period before humanity. The creations first alluded to, then, are not people, but something other than human beings. Job 38:4–7 refers to a time when "all the sons of God shouted for joy."

Who were these "sons of God"? They were not human beings; they were unquestionably angels and archangels, and the indirect inference is that God had put that former world under the charge of an archangel, Lucifer.

(b) Celestial Catastrophe

The Bible also alludes to a catastrophe before man was created, which makes the first two verses of Genesis 1 understandable. God gave the rule of this universe to Lucifer, who opposed himself to God's authority and rule. In falling, he dragged everything down with him, and consequently called forth on this earth a tremendous judgment which resulted in chaos— "the earth was without form, and void."

This catastrophe is referred to in such passages as Isaiah 14:12, "How you are fallen from heaven, O Lucifer, son of the morning!" and Luke 10:18, "I saw Satan fall like lightning from heaven." When did our Lord behold this? Surely it is legitimate to suggest that this refers to the period before our Lord's incarnation, when He was with God, in the beginning, before all things. (This particular verse is frequently thought to refer to the time yet to be, and that our Lord annihilated time by His foreknowledge.)

These verses are like mountain peaks revealing a whole table-land of God's revelation of the order of things before humanity was created. This interpretation is of the nature of a legitimate speculation and would seem to account for a great number of indications in the Bible. Beware, however, of making too much of these indications, because although as has been hinted, chaos may have been the result of judgment, a careful reading of Genesis 1:1–2 does not necessarily imply it.

(c) Celestial Condemnation

Then comes the condemnation of the angels, a celestial condemnation, the condemnation of Lucifer and all his angels, nothing whatsoever to do with humanity, "And the angels who did not keep their proper domain, but left their own abode, He has reserved in everlasting chains under darkness for the judgment of the great day" (Jude 6).

When Jesus Christ uses the phrase "from the beginning" He does not mean the beginning of humanity, but the very beginning of creation, which was long before man was created. (See John 8:44.) Hell is the place of angelic condemnation. It has nothing to do primarily with people. God's Book never says that hell was made for people, although it is true that it is the only place for the person who rejects God's salvation. Hell was the result of a distinct condemnation passed by God on celestial beings, and is as eternal as those celestial anarchists.

These three amazing episodes indicate the conditions before the creation of man, that is: that the archangels and the angels governed a wonderful world which God created in the beginning, and which God's Spirit alludes to in that phrase in Job 38:7, "When the morning stars sang together, and all the sons of God shouted for joy." Lucifer fell, and with him all his angels in a tremendous ruin. "And the earth was without form, and void; and darkness was upon the face of the deep. And the Spirit of God was hovering over the face of the waters" (Genesis 1:2).

Without some such explanation, verse 2 is unintelligible. To say that "In the beginning God created the heavens and the earth," and then to say that "the earth was without form, and void" is a confusion. The inference is that between the epochs referred to in these verses there occurred a catastrophe which the Bible does not say much about, the evident purpose of the Bible being to tell what God's purpose is with humanity. Roughly outlining that purpose, we might say that God created man in order to counteract the devil.

These sections refer to the strange unfamiliar background of the life we live at present. Such things are not to be made too much of, nor on the other hand are they to be ignored. It is necessary to note them in *Biblical Psychology* because they have a distinct part to play in humanity's present existence.

2. Conditions Leading to Man's Creation

You alone are the LORD; You have made heaven,
The heaven of heavens, with all their host,
The earth and everything on it,
The seas and all that is in them,

And You preserve them all.
The host of heaven worships You.

(Nehemiah 9:6)

(a) Terrestrial Chaos

Satan was the means of the ruin of the first created order, and now God begins to create another order out of the confusion of ruin. Void means the aftermath of destruction by judgment, or the result of Divine judgment.

(b) Terrestrial Creations

God began to create things. Genesis 1:2–25 gives a detailed account of the creation of the earth and the life upon it. The Bible nowhere says that God set processes to work and out of those processes evolved the things which now appear. The Bible says that God created things by a distinct act. If the Bible agreed with modern science, it would soon be out of date, because, in the very nature of things, modern science is bound to change.

Genesis 1 indicates that God created the earth and the life on the earth in order to fit the world for human beings.

(c) Terrestrial Cosmos

The order and beauty of this world were created by God for human beings. Genesis 1 verses 4, 10, 12, 18, 21, 25 and 31, all say that "God saw that it was good." After the judgment by God on the previous order, God created a new thing, for a totally new being whom no angel had ever seen.

This new being, man, stood at the end of the six days' work as a creature of earth, and he stood at the threshold of God's Sabbath Day. God created a unique being, not an angel, and not God Himself; He created a man. The man was created out of the earth, and related to the earth, and yet he was created in the image of God, whereby God could prove Himself more than a match for the devil by a creation a little lower than the angels, the order of beings to which Satan belongs.

This is, as it were, God's tremendous experiment in the creation of humanity. God put people at the head of the terrestrial creation. The whole meaning of the creation of the world was to fit and prepare a place for the wonderful being called *man* that God had in mind.

There is nothing in the Bible about the evolution and development of humanity as a survival of the fittest, or about the process of natural selection. The Bible reveals that we are earth and spirit, a combination of the two. The devil is spirit, just as God is; the angels are spirit; but when we come to the human being, he is earth and spirit.

3. Climax of Creation

(a) The Son of God

Adam is called the son of God. There is only one other "Son of God" in the Bible, and He is Jesus Christ.

Yet we are called "sons of God," but how? By being reinstated through the atonement of Jesus Christ. This is an important point. We are not the sons of God by natural generation. Adam did not come into the world as we do; neither did Adam come into the world as Jesus Christ came. Adam was not "begotten"; Jesus Christ was. Adam was "created." God created Adam, He did not beget him.

We are all generated, we are not created beings. Adam was the "son of God," and God created him as well as everything else that was created. In Genesis 1:27 we read, "So God created man in His own image, in the image of God He created him; male and female He created them." This is a point of importance. Adam and Eve are both needed before the image of God can be perfectly presented. God is, as it were, all that the best manhood presents us with, and all that the best womanhood presents us with. (This aspect will be dealt with in subsequent lectures.)

(b) The Six Days' Work

This word *day* means roughly what we understand by twenty-four hours, and has no such meaning as the Day of Atonement or the Day of Judgment.

Devotion to the ephemeral scientific doctrine of evolution is responsible for the endeavor to make out that the Bible means a period of years instead of a solar day. The particular unparabolic use of the term "morning and evening" in Genesis distinctly indicates a solar day. Man was the climax of the six days' work; in God's plan the whole of the six days' work of creation was for humans. The tendency nowadays is to put the six days' work of creation above people. Some people are far more concerned about dogs and cats than about human beings.

There is not only the tendency to exalt animals above people, but there is the speculation of the superman, which holds that the human being, as we understand him and as the Bible reveals him, is not the climax of creation, but that there is a higher being yet to be, called "the superman," and that the human being is as inferior to this being that is going to be as the ape is to the human.

All through the New Testament the Spirit of God has foretold that we are going to have the worship of man installed, and it is in our midst today. We are being told that Jesus Christ and God are ceasing to be of importance to modern men and women, and what we are worshiping more and more now is "Humanity," and this is slowly merging into a new phase; all the up-to-date minds are looking toward the manifestation of this "superman," a being much greater than the being we know as human.

Second Thessalonians 2:3–4 gives us a picture of the head of this great expectation. ". . . the son of perdition; who opposes

and exalts himself above all that is called God, or that is wor-
shiped, so that he sits as God in the temple of God, showing
himself that he is God." He is to be the darling of every religion;
there is to be a consolidation of religions, and of races and of
everything on the face of the earth, a great socialism.

The ethical standard of the superman claims to be higher
than Jesus Christ's standard. The tendency is noticeable already
in the objection of some people to Jesus Christ's teaching, such
as "You shall love your neighbor as yourself"; they say, "That is
selfish, you must love your neighbor and not think of yourself."
The doctrine of the superman is absolute sinless perfection. We
are going to evolve a being, they say, who has reached the place
where he cannot be tempted.

This is all an emanation from Satan. Man is the climax of
creation. He is on a stage a little lower than the angels, and God
is going to overthrow the devil by this being who is less than
angelic. God has, as it were, put the human being in the "open
field," and He is allowing the devil to do exactly what he likes
up to a certain point, "because," He says, "He who is in you is
greater than he who is in the world" (1 John 4:4).

This is also the explanation of our own spiritual setting.
Satan is to be humiliated by man, by the Spirit of God in man
through the wonderful regeneration of Jesus Christ.

Humanity, then, is the head and the purpose of the six days'
creation. The human body has in it those constituents that con-
nect it with the earth; it has fire and water and all the elements
of animal life; consequently God keeps us here. The earth is
humanity's domain, and we are going to be here again after the
terrestrial cremation. Hereafter, without the devil, without sin
and wrong. We are going to be here, marvelously redeemed in
this wonderful place which God made very beautiful, and with
which sin has played havoc, and creation itself is waiting "for
the revealing of the sons of God" (Romans 8:19).

(c) The Sabbath Rest

Not only is man the head and climax of the six days' work, but he is the beginning of, and stands at the threshold of, the Sabbath of God. God's heart is, as it were, absolutely at rest now that He has created man and woman; even in spite of the fact of the fall, and all else, God is absolutely confident that everything will turn out as He said it would. The devil has laughed at God's hope for thousands of years, and has ridiculed and scorned that hope, but God is not upset or alarmed about the final issue; He is certain that humankind will bruise the serpent's head. This has reference to those who are born again through Jesus Christ's amazing atonement.

2

MAN: HIS CREATION, CALLING, AND COMMUNION

Man's Making

1. **The Man of God's Making—Genesis 2:4–25**
   (a) The Image of God—John 4:24
   (b) The Image of God in Angels—Genesis 6:2; Psalm 89:6; Job 1:6; 38:7
   (c) The Image of God in Man—Genesis 1:26; Psalm 8:4–5
2. **The Manner of Man's Making—John 1:3**
   (a) Man's Body—Genesis 2:7
   (b) Man's Soul—Acts 17:28
   (c) Man's Self-Consciousness—Proverbs 20:27; 1 Corinthians 2:11[1]

---

1. N.B.: Visible creations that surround man are not in the image of God. Some notes will be given on the appearances of angels in our material universe. Some notes also on the human representations of God.

1. The Man of God's Making

God's heart is, so to speak, at rest now that He has created man (see Genesis 2:4–25).

(a) The Image of God

"God is Spirit" (John 4:24). This is a mountain-peak text which reveals a whole tableland of God's revelation about Himself.

(b) The Image of God in Angels

"Now there was a day when the sons of God came to present themselves before the LORD, and Satan also came among them" (Job 1:6). (See also Genesis 6:2; Psalm 89:6; Job 38:7.) The phrase "sons of God" in the Old Testament always refers to angels, and we have to find out from the context whether they are fallen angels or not. Angels have no physical frame, they are not like men and women, and they are not manifested after this order of things; since, however, they are called "sons of God," the inference is clear that they bear the image of God.

(c) The Image of God in Man

"Then God said, Let Us make man in Our image, according to Our likeness" (Genesis 1:26; see also Psalm 8:4–5). In its primary reference the image of God in man is to the hidden or interior life of the person. The image of God in the individual is primarily spiritual, yet it has to be manifested in his body also. "Thou hast made him but little lower than God," or "than the angels" (Psalm 8:5).

Man's chief glory and dignity is that he was made "of the earth, earthy" to manifest the image of God in that substance. We are apt to think that to be made of the earth is our humiliation, but it is the very point of which God's Word makes most. God "formed man of the dust of the ground," and the Redemption is for the dust of the ground as well as for the human spirit.

The human body before it degenerated must have been dazzling with light. We get this by inference from Genesis 3:7, "Then the eyes of both of them were opened, and they knew that they were naked; and they sewed fig leaves together, and made themselves coverings." Man and woman were obviously naked before their disobedience, and the death of their union with God was instantly revealed in their bodies. (We shall deal with this point in the next chapter.)

From these revelation facts in God's Book, people have reasoned backwards; they have said that because men and women have bodies, therefore God has a corporality too. This error began centuries ago and is continually being revived. The Bible does speak of the "form" of God—"Who, being in the form of God" (Philippians 2:6); but the error has arisen from our too readily inferring that "form" means physical body.

In the Old Testament there are allusions over and over again to what is called the *anthropomorphic* view of God; that is, God is represented as having hands and limbs and looking like a man, and from this it is easy to draw the inference that God has a body like a human being. All these Old Testament pictures of God are forecasts of the Incarnation. There are passages in the book of Isaiah which reveal apparently conflicting statements about God. He is represented in many contradictory phrases; but all these contradictions blend in that unique Being, Jesus Christ, the last Adam. The great triune God has "form," and the term that is used for describing that form is *glory*.

"And now, O Father, glorify Me together with Yourself, with the glory which I had with You before the world was" (John 17:5). Our word *Trinity* is an attempt to convey the externally disclosed divine nature, and *glory* is the Bible term for conveying the idea of the external form of that triune Being. (This will be alluded to several times in the course of our studies in

Biblical Psychology, and we shall thus become familiar with this profound revelation.)

God is sometimes referred to as the sun, but the sun is never stated to be made in the image of God, although there are illustrations of God in God's Book drawn from the sun. But nowhere is it stated that God made the sun in His own image. In the Bible record angels certainly did appear to individuals. We may take it from the revealed facts in God's Word that angels have the power of will to materialize and to appear to people when people are in suitable subjective conditions. This power is given to good and bad angels alike. It is probably to this that Paul refers in Ephesians 6:12: "For we do not wrestle against flesh and blood, but against principalities, against powers, against the rulers of the darkness of this age, against spiritual hosts of wickedness in the heavenly places."

This inference is a great guide in regard to spiritualism. Spiritualism, according to the Bible, is not a trick; it is a fact. A person can communicate with beings of a different order from his own, and can put himself into a state of subjectivity in which angels can appear.

2. The Manner of Man's Making

(a) Man's Body

"All things were made through Him, and without Him nothing was made that was made" (John 1:3). God did not create human beings by direct fiat; He molded the man and the woman by His own deliberate power. (See Genesis 1:26–27.) A common mistake is to infer that the soul was made along with the body; the Bible says that the body was created prior to the soul. Adam's body was formed by God "of the dust of the ground"; which means that humanity is constituted to have affinity with everything on this earth.

This is not humanity's calamity but its peculiar dignity. We do not further our spiritual lives in spite of our bodies, but in and by means of our bodies.

(b) Man's Soul

Then we read that God "breathed into his nostrils the breath of life; and man became a living being," a soul-enlivened nature. There is another "breathing" mentioned in John 20:22, when our risen Lord breathed on the disciples and said, "Receive the Holy Spirit." This has not the same meaning as Genesis 2:7, where God breathed into the man's nostrils the breath of life which became, not God's Spirit, but the human spirit.

Jesus Christ breathed into His disciples Holy Spirit, and the human spirit became energized by the Spirit of the Son of God. When God breathed into Adam's nostrils the breath of life, Adam did not become a living God, he became "a living being." Consequently in human beings, regenerate or degenerate, there are three aspects—spirit, soul, and body.

(c) Man's Self-Consciousness

The uniting of human personality, spirit, soul, and body, may be brought about in various ways. The Bible reveals that sensuality will do it (Ephesians 5:5); that drunkenness will do it (Ephesians 5:18); and that the devil will do it (Luke 11:21). But the Holy Spirit alone will do it rightly; this is the only true at-one-ment. When our personalities are sanctified, it is not God's Spirit that is sanctified, it is our spirits. "Now may the God of peace Himself sanctify you completely; and may your whole spirit, soul, and body be preserved blameless at the coming of our Lord Jesus Christ" (1 Thessalonians 5:23).

Paul's injunction to "cleanse ourselves from all filthiness of the flesh and spirit" refers to the human spirit. God's inbreathing into Adam's nostrils the breath of life called into actual existence his soul, which was potentially in the body, that is, existing in possibility. A person's soul is neither his body nor his spirit, it is that creation which holds his spirit and his body together, and is the medium of expressing his spirit in his body.

It is not true to state that one's soul molds his body; it is his spirit that molds his body, and soul is the medium his spirit uses to express itself. It is impossible for us to conceive what Adam was like as God made him—his material body instinct with spiritual light, his flesh in the likeness of God, his soul in absolute harmony with God, and his spirit in the image of God.

In the personal life of a person who has fallen away from God, his soul and his spirit gravitate more and more to the dust of the earth, more and more to the brutish life on one side and the satanic life on the other. The marvelous revelation is that in and through Jesus Christ, the personality in its three aspects of body, soul, and spirit, is sanctified and preserved blameless in this dispensation; and in another dispensation, body, soul and spirit will be instinct with the glory of God.

Whenever an Old Testament saint succeeded in perfectly doing God's will, earth seemed to lose its hold on him, for example, Enoch, Elijah.

Again, why did not Jesus Christ go straight back to heaven from the Mount of Transfiguration? He was standing in the full blaze and glory of His pre-incarnate glory; but He "emptied Himself" a second time of the glory of God, and came down from the Mount to the humiliation of the Cross. When Jesus Christ comes again, those who are saved and sanctified will be "changed—in a moment, in the twinkling of an eye"; all disharmony will cease and a new order will begin.

What does glorification mean? Adam is never spoken of as being glorified in the first decades of creation. Glorification is Christ enthroned in fullness of consummating power, when having subdued all things for Himself, He enters back into

Absolute Deity as "in the beginning" before any creations were. (See 1 Corinthians 15:28.) That is where our vocabulary will not go.

To sum up: God made man in His own image and breathed into his nostrils the breath of life, and the human being became, not a living God, but a living being, a soul-enlivened nature; his whole bodily temple, every corpuscle of blood, every nerve, every sinew, was the temple which could manifest harmony with God—manifest the image of God in the human form through faith and love. The angels can manifest the image of God only in bodiless spirits; only one being can manifest God on this earth, and that is the human. Satan thwarted God's purpose, and then laughed his devilish laugh against God, but the Bible says that God will laugh last. "The LORD laughs at him, for He sees that his day is coming" (Psalm 37:13).

3

MAN: HIS CREATION, CALLING, AND COMMUNION

Man's Unmaking

1. **The Primal Anarchy—Genesis 3; Romans 5:12**
   (a) The Serpent—Genesis 3:1
   (b) The Serpent and Eve—2 Corinthians 11:3
   (c) The Serpent, Eve and Adam—1 Timothy 2:14
   Original Sin—Doing without God
2. **The Pre-Adamic Anarchy—Ezekiel 28:12–15**
   (a) Satanic Pretensions, Implied—Matthew 4:8;
   2 Corinthians 4:4
   (b) Satanic Perversions—Genesis 3:5; implied, Job 1:9
   (c) Satanic Perils—Jude 6; Matthew 16:23; 2 Thessalonians
   2:9
   Origin of Sin—Dethroning of God

3. The Punished Anarchists—Genesis 3:23–24
   (a) Destitution and Death—Genesis 2:17
   (b) Division from Deity—Genesis 3:8, 13
   (c) Divine Declaration—Genesis 3:15
       Origin of Salvation—Daring way back to God

Now we come to the revelation statement of how sin was introduced into this world.

1. The Primal Anarchy

(a) The Serpent

"Now the serpent was more cunning than any beast of the field which the LORD God had made" (Genesis 3:1). This creature was evidently a beautiful creation of God's and we must beware of imagining that it was in the beginning as it was after being cursed. After the fall, God cursed this beautiful creature into the serpent, to feed on dust and to crawl. The serpent in the physical domain is a picture of Satan in the spiritual domain. In our universe of physical things we shall find many which picture spiritual things. (This line of thought belongs to Biblical Philosophy, so it is only alluded to in passing.)

(b) The Serpent and Eve

"But I fear, lest somehow, as the serpent deceived Eve by his craftiness, so your minds may be corrupted from the simplicity that is in Christ" (2 Corinthians 11:3). Why did Satan come by way of the serpent, and to Eve? Why did he not go directly to Adam?

In thinking of man and woman as they were first created, it is extremely difficult, especially nowadays, to present the subject without introducing small, petty and disreputable ideas relative to the distinctions between man and woman. In Adam and Eve we are dealing with the primal creations of God.

Adam was created immediately by the hand of God; Eve was created mediately. Eve stands for the soul side, the psychic side, of the human creation; all her sympathies, and affinities were with the other creations of God around. Adam stands for the spirit side, the kingly, Godward side.

Adam and Eve together are the likeness of God, "Then God said, 'Let Us make man in Our image,' . . . male and female, He created them" (Genesis 1:26–27). The revelation made here is not that woman stands as inferior to man, but that she stands in quite a different relation to all things, and that both man and woman are required for the complete creation of God referred to by the general term *Man*.

(c) The Serpent, Eve, and Adam

"And Adam was not deceived, but the woman being deceived fell into transgression" (1 Timothy 2:14). Eve, having this affinity and sympathy with the other creations around, would naturally listen with more unsuspecting interest to the suggestions which came through the cunning creature which spoke to her. The Bible says that Eve was deceived, it does not say that Adam was deceived; consequently Adam is far more responsible than Eve because he sinned deliberately.

There was no conscious intention to disobey in Eve's heart, she was deceived by the cunning wisdom of Satan via the serpent. Adam, however, was not deceived, he sinned with a deliberate understanding of what he was doing, so the Bible associates "sin" with Adam ("Therefore, just as through one man sin entered into the world."—Romans 5:12) and "transgression" with Eve ("And Adam was not deceived, but the woman being deceived fell into the transgression"—1 Timothy 2:14).

In this connection it is of importance to note that the Bible reveals that our Redeemer entered into the world through the woman. Man, as man, had no part whatsoever in the Redemption of the world; it was "the seed of the woman." In Protestant theology and in the Protestant outlook we have suffered much from our opposition to the Roman Catholic Church on this one point, that is, intense antipathy to Mariolatry, and we have lost the meaning of the woman side of the revelation of God.

All that we understand by womanhood and by manhood, all that we understand by fatherhood and motherhood, is embraced in the term *El Shaddai* (Genesis 17:1; 19). (This is a mere hint at a line of thought that cannot be taken up here.)

A distinction may legitimately be made between transgression and sin (see Matthew 6:12–15). Transgression is nearly always an unconscious act, there is no conscious determination to do wrong. Sin is never an unconscious act, as far as culpability is concerned, it is always a conscious determination. Adam was the introducer of sin into this order of things (see Romans 5:12). Original sin is doing without God.

A noticeable feature in the conduct of Adam and Eve is that when God turned them out of the garden, they did not rebel. The characteristic of sin in human beings is fear and shame. Sin in human beings is doing without God, but it is not rebellion against God in its first stages.

2. The Pre-Adamic Anarchy
(a) Satanic Pretensions

The pretensions of Satan are clear. He is the god of this world and he will not allow relationship to the true God. Satan's attitude is that of a pretender to the throne, he claims it as his right. Wherever and whenever the rule of God is recognized by people, Satan proceeds to instill the tendency of mutiny and rebellion and lawlessness.

(b) Satanic Perversions

Satan ever perverts what God says. Genesis 3:5 is one of the revelation facts concerning Satan: "For God knows that in the day you eat of it, your eyes will be opened, and you will be like God, knowing good and evil." Remember, the characteristics of human union with God are faith in God and love for Him. This union was the first thing Satan aimed at in Adam and Eve, and he did it by perverting what God had said.

In the case of Job, Satan goes the length of trying to pervert God's idea of humanity. That is an amazing revelation of the power of Satan! He presents himself with the sons of God in the very presence of God, trying to pervert God's mind about Job. We might apply personally (not exegetically) this statement from Isaiah: "A bruised reed He will not break, and smoking flax He will not quench" (Isaiah 42:3).

Satan is called "the accuser of our brethren" (Revelation 12:10); he not only slanders God to us, but accuses us to God. It is as if he looked down and pointed out a handful of people and insinuated to God, "Now, that woman is a perfect disgrace to You, she has only one spark of grace among all the fibers of her life; I advise You to stamp out that spark." What is the revelation? "He will raise it to a flame."

Or, he points out a person and says, "That person is a disgrace to You, he is a 'bruised reed,' I wonder You build any hope on him whatsoever, he is a hindrance and an upset to You, break him!" But no, the Lord will bind him up and make him into a wonderful instrument. The old reeds were used to make wonderful musical instruments, and instead of crushing out the life that is bruised and wrong, God heals it and discourses sweet music through it.

In the revelation in Genesis 3, Satan implies that God is jealous—"God knows that if you disobey Him you will become as God." Satan perverted God's statement. He did not say that

God had said it, he was too wise for that, he said, "Has God indeed said . . . ?" insinuating "You do not know what God meant, but I do; He means that if you disobey Him and eat of the tree, you will become as He is."

I do not think that Eve accepted this suggestion about God, because, if you watch, Satan's words worked in her as a deception unconsciously, all she saw was that the fruit was "pleasant to the eyes." Our discernment of what Eve did is given to us by the Spirit of God. We are not ignorant of Satan's devices (2 Corinthians 2:11). Satan's pretension is that he is equal with God. His perversion is twofold: he tries to pervert what God says to us, and also to pervert God's mind about us.

(c) Satanic Perils

"And the angels who did not keep their proper domain, but left their own abode, He has reserved in everlasting chains under darkness for the judgment of the great day" (Jude 6). What are satanic perils? The satanic perils spring straight out of the way we are made, and in Matthew 16:22–23 we come to where we live. Have you ever noticed the remarkable identification Jesus Christ makes in this passage? When Peter said, "Far be it from You, Lord," what did our Lord reply?—"Get behind Me, Satan" (Matthew 16). Our Lord then told Peter that what he had said belonged to the wrong disposition in humanity, which He identifies with Satan.

Beware of satanic perils when they are taken to be merely natural tendencies. Remember, Satan is an awful being, he is able to deceive us on the right hand and on the left, and the first beginnings of his deceptions are along the lines of self-pity. Self-pity, self-conceit, and self-sympathy will make us accept slanders against God. Satanic perils arise out of the wrong disposition which was introduced into the human race, and that wrong disposition shows itself in self-pity and self-sympathy.

Beware of slandering the "old man," as is often done; I mean, beware of making the old man appear ugly. The old man does not appear ugly to anyone but the Holy Spirit. The old man— the disposition that connects me with the mystical body of sin, is a highly desirable thing until I am quickened by the Spirit of God and born from above; it makes me consider my rights, it makes me look after myself and consider what is good for me. "You are those who justify yourselves before men, but God knows your hearts. For what is highly esteemed among men is an abomination in the sight of God" (Luke 16:15).

"Then the lawless one will be revealed . . . . The coming of the lawless one is according to the working of Satan, with all power signs, and lying wonders" (2 Thessalonians 2:8–9). These verses reveal another peril, that is, that there are tremendous and appalling external manifestations of Satan. The curious thing nowadays is that people are watching eagerly for these manifestations of satanic power while they allow other satanic perils, such as spiritualism, to have their way.

Once the disposition is altered, we shall never be deluded by any of the satanic powers which manifest themselves in the external world.

The great peril is the peril within, which people never think of as a peril. My right to myself, self-pity, self-conceit, consideration for my progress, my ways of looking at things, those things are the satanic perils which will keep us in perfect sympathy with Satan. Satanic anarchy is conscious and determined opposition to God. Wherever God's rule is made known, Satan will put himself alongside and oppose it.

Satan's sin is at the summit of all sins; people's sin is at the foundation of all sins, and there is all the difference in the world between them. Satan's sin is conscious, emphatic, and immortal rebellion against God; he has no fear, no veneration, and no respect for God's rule. Whenever God's law is stated, that is sufficient, Satan will break it, and his whole purpose is to get people to do the same. Satanic anarchy is a conscious, tremendous thing.

Satan is never represented in the Bible as being guilty of doing wrong *things*: he is a wrong *being*. People are responsible for doing wrong things, and they do wrong things because of the wrong disposition in them. The moral cunning of our nature makes us blame Satan when we know perfectly well we should blame ourselves; the true blame for sins lies in the wrong disposition in us. In all probability Satan is as much upset as the Holy Spirit is when people fall in external sin, but for a different reason. When people go into external sin and upset their lives, Satan knows perfectly well that they will want another Ruler, a Savior and Deliverer; as long as Satan can keep people in peace and unity and harmony apart from God, he will do so. (See Luke 11:21–22.)

Remember, then, Satan's sin is dethroning God.

3. The Punished Anarchists

(a) Destitution and Death

We have seen in chapter 2 how God punished Satan; He has reserved for him what is revealed as the eternal hell. Now we come to the punishment of Adam and Eve.

"Therefore the LORD God sent him out of the garden of Eden to till the ground from which he was taken. So He drove out the man . . ." (Genesis 3:23–24). It is a familiar revelation fact to us that there was no rebellion in Adam and Eve. They did not fight against God, they simply went out of the garden covered with fear and shame. Satan was the originator of sin; Adam was not. Adam accepted the way Eve had been deceived and sinned with his eyes open, and instantly an extraordinary thing happened: "they knew that they were naked."

There is quite sufficient evidence to indicate that when

Adam's spirit, soul, and body were united in perfect faith and love to God, his soul was the medium through which the marvelous life of the Spirit of God was brought down. The very image of God was brought down into his material body and it was clothed in an inconceivable splendor of light until the whole person was in the likeness of God.

The moment he disobeyed, the connection with God was shut off, and spirit, soul, and body tumbled into death that instant. The fact of dissolving into dust in a few years' time is nothing more than death visible. Do not bring the idea of time in at all. Death happened instantly in spirit, soul, and body, spiritually and psychically. The connecting link with deity was gone, and the human spirit, soul, and body tumbled into disintegrating death; and when they "heard the sound of the LORD God walking in the garden" (Genesis 3:8), they were terrified and hid themselves.

By the term *death* is meant that the body crumbles back into dust, the soul disappears, and the spirit goes back to God who gave it. (See Ecclesiastes 12:7.) Spirit is the immortal part of the human being. The spirit of a person is not absorbed into God, it goes back to God, who breathed into his nostrils the breath of life, with the characteristics upon it which he has developed for either the judgment or the praise of God.

God turned human beings out of the garden of Eden into destitution, but in turning them out He put them on the way to become infinitely grander and nobler beings than even Adam was at the first. The whole Bible, from Genesis to Revelation, instead of being a picture of despair is the very opposite. The worst is always bettered by God. God, as it were, took His hand off humanity and let Satan do the very worst that diabolical spiritual genius could do.

Satan knew what would happen, he knew that God would have to punish humanity, and God did punish, but with the perfect certainty that the being that was to come out of the ordeal of the fall would be greater than the first Adam. Adam and Eve went out from the garden covered with fear and shame.

In the New Testament the characteristics of the wrong disposition are fearfulness and unbelief; what does the atonement do? It takes away fearfulness and unbelief, and brings us back again into the relationship of faith and love to God. ". . . faith and love which are in Christ Jesus" (1 Timothy 1:14).

Regeneration means that the Holy Spirit lifts a person out of the pit he is in through sin and death into a totally new realm, and by sudden intuitions and impulses the new life is able to lift up soul and body. The soul must obey the union with God which the new life has given, or it may ultimately fall away. The new birth will bring us to the place where spirit, soul, and body are identified with Christ, sanctified here and now and preserved in that condition, not by intuitions now, not by sudden impulses and marvelous workings of the new life within, but by a conscious, superior, moral integrity, transfigured through and through by our union with God through the atonement.

(b) Division from Deity

When Adam sinned his union with God was cut off, and God turned him out of the garden and guarded the way to the tree of life, that is to say, God prevented Adam from getting back as a fallen being. If Adam had gotten back to the tree of life as a fallen being, he would have become an incarnate devil, and God would have been finally thwarted with humanity; but when Adam was driven out, God placed cherubim and a gleaming sword to keep the way of the tree of life. If Adam had become an incarnate devil, there would have been the same havoc on this earth as when the angels fell; but Adam did not sin as Satan sinned. Adam was covered with fear and shame, and the light that had glistened all through his physical body faded out because of sin.

Jesus Christ is going to change "our lowly body" and conform it "to His glorious body" (Philippians 3:21) and the result will be not an intuitive innocence only, but a conscious manly and womanly holiness. *Holiness* is the expression of the new disposition God has given us maintained against all odds. Holiness is militant, Satan is continually pressing and ardent, but holiness maintains itself. It is morality on fire and transfigured into the likeness of God. Holiness is not only what God gives me, but what I manifest that God has given me.

I manifest this brilliant holiness by my reaction against sin, the world, and the devil. Wherever God's saints are in the world they are protected by a wall of fire which they do not see, but Satan does. "The wicked one does not touch him" (1 John 5:18). Satan has to ask and plead for permission; as to whether God grants him permission is to do with the sovereignty of God and is not in our domain to understand. All we know is that Jesus Christ taught us to pray, "Do not lead us into temptation."

(c) Divine Declaration

Adam was turned out into destitution, and was thus divided from deity; God disappeared from him, and he disappeared from God. As mentioned before, there are three false unities possible in a person's experience, that is, sensuality, drunkenness, and the devil, whereby a person's spirit, soul, and body are brought into harmony and he is quite peaceful, quite happy, with no sense of death about him. A drunken individual has no self-consciousness, he is perfectly delivered from all the things which disintegrate and upset. Sensuality and Satan will do the same; but each of these unities is only possible for a time. When Satan rules, people's souls are in peace, they are not troubled or upset like others, but quite happy and peaceful.

There is only one right at-one-ment, and that is in Jesus Christ; only one right unity, and that is when body, soul, and spirit are united to God by the Holy Spirit through the marvelous atonement of the Lord Jesus Christ. The origin of salvation is a daring way back to God.

How did Jesus Christ make a way back to God? Through every worst onslaught of Satan. By the sheer force of the tremendous integrity of His incarnation, Jesus Christ hewed a way straight through sin and death and hell right back to God, more than conqueror over all.

As in chapters 1 and 2, we are dealing here more properly with theology than with psychology, but it is these fundamental theological facts which must safeguard our psychological studies.

4

MAN: HIS CREATION, CALLING, AND COMMUNION

Readjustment by Redemption

1. **Incarnation—Word Made Flesh—John 1:14**
   God-man
   (a) Self-Surrender of Trinity—John 17:5; Mark 13:32;
       Ephesians 4:10
   (b) Self-same with Trinity—Matthew 2:27; John 14:9
   (c) Self-sufficiency of Trinity—Proverbs 8:22–32
2. **Identification—Son Made Sin—2 Corinthians 5:20–21**
   God and Man
   (a) Day of His Death—Matthew 16:21; Mark 9:31;
       Romans 6:3
   (b) Day of His Resurrection—Romans 6:5; Philippians 3:10
   (c) Day of His Ascension—Matthew 28:18; 2 Corinthians
       5:16

3. **Invasion—Sinner Made Saint—Galatians 2:20**
   God in Man
   (a) The New Man—2 Corinthians 5:17
   (b) The New Manners—Ephesians 4:22–32
   (c) The New Mankind—Ephesians 4:13; 2 Peter 3:10

1. Incarnation—Word Made Flesh

The Word became flesh and dwelt among us. (John
1:14)

The word *Trinity* is not a Bible word. Over and over again in
the Bible the triune God is revealed, so that the idea conveyed by
the Trinity is thoroughly Scriptural. The following distinctions
have existed from all eternity: The Essence of Godhead (*esse*)
usually known as God the Father; The Existence of Godhead
(*existere*) usually known as God the Son; The Proceeding of
Godhead (*procedere*) usually known as God the Holy Spirit.

One thing we have to guard against is the teaching that God
became incarnate in order to realize Himself; it is an unbiblical statement. God was self-sufficient before the Son became
incarnate. What is known as New Theology springs from this
fundamental error—that God had to create something in order
to realize Himself; consequently we are told that we are essential to God's existence, that apart from us, God is not. If we
start with that theory, then all that goes by the name of New
Theology follows easily. The Bible has nothing to do with such
conceptions.

The Creation and the Incarnation are the outgoings of
the overflowing life of the Godhead. Another aspect of New
Theology is that God is all; the Bible reveals that God is not
all. The Bible distinctly states that our universe is *pluralistic*, not
monistic; that means there are other forces at work besides God,
that is, humanity and the devil. These are not God, and never

will be. Humanity is meant to come back to God and to be in harmony with Him through Jesus Christ; the devil will be at enmity with God forever.

In Philippians 2:6 the "form" of God is mentioned. What is the form of God? In chapter 2 we found that people have reasoned that because the human being was made in the image of God, therefore God has a body. We stated that this did not mean God has a corporeal form, and that whenever bodily members are mentioned in connection with God, the reference is to the Incarnation. The Godhead had a form originally, and that form is best implied by the term *glory*.

The Bible reveals that the Godhead was absolutely self-sufficient. God did not need to be incarnated in order to realize Himself; neither was the creation needed to enable God to realize Himself. Jesus Christ is not a Being one-half God and one-half human. When George Eliot translated David Strauss's *Life of Jesus*, this impossibility to human reason was presented to her mind, and it was along this line that she made shipwreck of her faith.

(a) Self-surrender of the Trinity

The Bible reveals that Jesus Christ is God-man, that is, God Incarnate, the Godhead existing in flesh and blood. The Incarnation is part of the self-surrender of the Trinity. John 17:5 refers to this. "And now, O Father, glorify Me together with Yourself, with the glory which I had with You before the world was." Jesus Christ was not a Being who became divine; He was the Godhead incarnated, the Word made weak. Jesus Christ emphatically alludes to His own limitations, and Paul says He "emptied Himself" (Philippians 2:7 KJV), that is, of the form of God, "taking the form of a bondservant, and coming in the likeness of men."

In Mark 13:32 we see another indication of the limitations

of our Lord. "But of that day and hour no one knows, not even the angels in heaven, nor the Son, but only the Father." I am aware of the danger of attempting to sketch out the self-consciousness of Jesus; we cannot do it. We have to remember what the Scriptures say about Him—that He was the Godhead incarnate, and that He emptied Himself of His glory in becoming incarnate. In the redemption, it was not God the Son paying a price to God the Father: it was God the Father, God the Son, and God the Holy Spirit surrendering this marvelous Being, the Lord Jesus Christ, for one definite purpose. Never separate the incarnation from the atonement. The incarnation is for the sake of the atonement. In dealing with the incarnation, we are dealing with a revelation fact, not with a speculation.

We find another allusion to the limitations of Jesus through His incarnation in the epistle to the Hebrews. To say that Jesus Christ could not be tempted flatly contradicts the Word of God—He was "in all points tempted like as we are, yet without sin" (Hebrews 4:15).

(b) Self-same with Trinity

"All things have been delivered to Me by My Father, and no one knows the Son except the Father. Nor does anyone know the Father except the Son, and the one to whom the Son wills to reveal Him" (Matthew 11:27). Jesus says here, in effect, "I am the only medium for revealing the Father; you cannot know the Father through nature, or through the love of your friends, you cannot know the Father in any other way than through Me."

Couple with that verse our Lord's words in John 14:6, 9, "I am the way, the truth, and the life. No one comes to the Father except through Me . . . . He who has seen Me has seen the Father; so how can you say, 'Show us the Father?'" where He makes the same statement. No one knows anything about the Father unless he accepts the revelation made of Him by Jesus

Christ. These statements come over and over again, and if we examine our Lord's teaching closely we shall find that He makes the final destiny of man depend on his relationship to Himself.

(c) The Self-sufficiency of the Trinity

Read in the light of the incarnation this passage is amazing. What Solomon calls "Wisdom" is the same word as *Logos* in John 1; it means God's Word expressing His thought. The Trinity was self-sufficient; the incarnation was not meant to satisfy God, but for another purpose altogether. The thought is exactly the opposite, that is, instead of people being necessary to complement God so that He might realize Himself, the incarnation was in order that people might realize God and gain adjustment to Him. The whole purpose of the incarnation is redemption, that is, to overcome the disasters of the fall and produce a being more noble than the original Adam. At the climax of everything, the Son resumes His original position in the Trinity; the Son gives up all to the Father, and the Trinity thus resolves itself again into this absolute self-sufficient Deity. (See 1 Corinthians 15:28.)

2. Identification—Son Made Sin

We implore you on Christ's behalf, be reconciled to God. For He made Him who knew no sin to be sin for us, that we might become the righteousness of God in Him. (2 Corinthians 5:20–21)

These verses reveal why God became incarnate, why the Word was made weak, why the Logos became possessed of a weak human frame, that is, that the Son might be identified with sin. The revelation is not that Jesus Christ was punished for our sins, that is a slighter aspect. The statement in verse 21 is astounding: He was made to be sin for us. Jesus Christ became identified not only with the disposition of sin, but with the very body of sin. He who had no sin, no connection in Himself with the body of sin, became identified with sin, He made Him who knew no sin to be sin (2 Corinthians 5:21).

Language can hardly bear the strain put upon it, but it may nevertheless convey the thought that Jesus Christ went straight through identification with sin in order that every man and woman on earth might be freed from sin through the atonement. He went through the depths of damnation, through the deepest depths of death and hell, and came out more than conqueror; consequently anyone and everyone who is willing to be identified with Him will find that he or she is freed from the disposition of sin, freed from the connection with the body of sin, and that he or she too can come out more than conqueror because of what Jesus Christ has done.

(a) The Day of His Death

> He taught His disciples and said to them, "The Son of Man is being betrayed into the hands of men, and they will kill Him. And after He is killed, He will rise the third day." (Mark 9:31; see also Matthew 16:21; Romans 6:3)

By *day* we mean the period of time covered by our Lord's life on earth. Why was He born as a Babe in such conditions that the mightiest empires of the world were simply not able to detect His existence? Why did He live those thirty years in Nazareth, and those three years of popularity, scandal, and hatred, and why did He say He came on purpose to lay down His life? Our Lord never presented His death as that of a martyr. He said, "I have power to lay it [My life] down, and I have power to take it again" (John 10:18). He laid down His life because of the great purpose behind in the mind of God.

The only way we can explain Jesus Christ is the way He explains Himself—and He never explains Himself away. Why did Jesus Christ live and die? The Scriptures reveal that He lived and died and rose again that we might be readjusted to the Godhead—that we might be delivered from sin and be brought back into the relationship of favor with God.

If we teach that Jesus Christ cannot deliver from sin we shall end in nothing short of blasphemy. Present that line of thinking before God, tell Him that the atonement cannot deliver us from sin but can only give us a divine anticipation, and the danger and unscripturalness of it will soon appear.

The Bible reveals that Jesus Christ became identified with sin in order that "we might become the righteousness of God in Him" (2 Corinthians 5:21). Forgiveness is a tremendous thing from our standpoint, but it is not the whole experimental meaning of the atonement for us. We can become so identified with Jesus Christ until we know that "our old man was crucified with Him" (Romans 6:6), that is, that our connection with the body of sin is severed, and we may become "the righteousness of God in Him" (2 Corinthians 5:21). This means we are readjusted to God and are free to fulfill all His commands.

(b) The Day of His Resurrection

"For if we have been united together in the likeness of His death, certainly we also shall be in the likeness of His resurrection" (Romans 6:5; see also Philippians 3:10). By His resurrection, Jesus Christ has power to impart to us the Holy Spirit, which means a totally new life. The Holy Spirit is the Deity in proceeding power who applies the atonement of the Son of God in our experience. Jesus Christ laid all the emphasis on the coming of the Holy Spirit—"When He, the Spirit of truth, has come, He will guide you into all truth" (John 16:13), "and bring to your remembrance all things that I said to you" (John 14:26); He will not only be with you, but He "shall be in you."

We hear on the right hand and on the left that this is the age of the Holy Spirit. Thank God it is, and the Holy Spirit is with all men and women that they might receive Him. Just as God the Father was rejected and spurned in the Old Testament dispensation, and Jesus Christ the Son was despised and spurned in His dispensation, so God the Holy Spirit is despised (as well as flattered), in this dispensation. He is not given His right; we praise Him and say that we rely on His power, but the question of receiving Him that He may make real *in* us all that Jesus Christ did *for* us, is a rare experience.

As soon as the Holy Spirit comes in as life and as light, He will chase through every avenue of our minds; His light will penetrate every recess of our hearts; He will chase His light through every affection of our souls, and make us know what sin is. The Holy Spirit convicts of sin, humanity does not. The Holy Spirit is that marvelous Spirit that kept our Lord when He was incarnate—spirit, soul, and body—in perfect harmony with absolute Deity.

When Jesus said "You have no life in you," He meant the life He lived; and we cannot have that life saving through Him. He who believes on the Son has everlasting life (see John 3:16)—the life Jesus lived, Holy Spirit life. The Holy Spirit will take us, spirit, soul, and body, and bring us back into communion with God; and if we obey the light He gives, He will lead us into identification with the death of Jesus until we know experientially that our old man, my right to myself, is crucified with Him and our human nature is free now to obey the commands of God.

The word *substitution* is never used in the Bible, although the idea is a Scriptural one. Substitution is always twofold—not only is Jesus Christ identified with my sin, but I am so identified with Him that the disposition which ruled Him is in me.

(c) The Day of His Ascension

"And Jesus came and spoke to them saying, 'All authority has been given to Me in heaven and on earth'" (Matthew 28:18; see also 2 Corinthians 5:16). At His ascension our Lord became omnipresent, omniscient and omnipotent. This means that all He was in the days of His flesh, all that He was able to impart in the day of His resurrection, He is now almighty to bestow without measure on all obedient human beings. Jesus Christ makes us one in holiness with Himself, one in love with Himself, and ultimately one in glory with Himself. He is the supreme Sovereign, and He is able to give to His people a supreme sovereignty. In the days of our flesh, He says, "Lo, I am with you always, even to the end of the age" (Matthew 28:20). He is with us in all power and in all wisdom, guiding, directing, controlling, and subduing. He is King of kings and Lord of lords from the day of His ascension until now.

3. Invasion—Sinner Made Saint

I have been crucified with Christ, it is no longer I who live, but Christ lives in me: and the life which I now live in the flesh I live by faith in the Son of God, who loved me and gave Himself up for me. (Galatians 2:20)

Through the identification of Jesus Christ with sin we can be brought back again into perfect harmony with God; but God does not take away our responsibility; He puts upon us a new responsibility. We are made sons and daughters of God through the atonement and we have a tremendous dignity to maintain; we have no business to bow our necks to any yoke saving the yoke of the Lord Jesus Christ. There ought to be in us a holy scorn whenever it comes to being dictated to by the spirit of the age in which we live.

The age in which we live is governed by the prince of this world who hates Jesus Christ. His great doctrine is self-realization. We ought to be free from the dominion of the prince of this world; only one yoke should be upon our shoulders, the yoke of the Lord Jesus.

(a) The New Man

Our Lord was meek toward His Father. He let God Almighty do what He liked with His life and never murmured; He never awakened self-pity, nor brought down sympathy for Himself. "Take My yoke upon you, and learn from Me, for I am gentle and lowly in heart, and you will find rest for your souls. For My yoke is easy and My burden is light" (Matthew 11:29–30).

Galatians 2:20 is the Scriptural expression of identification with Jesus Christ in such a way that the whole life is changed. The destiny was becoming wonderfully like the destiny of Satan, that is, self-realization; now, Paul says, it is no longer the destiny of self-realization for me, but the destiny of Christ-realization ("and the life which I now live in the flesh I live by faith in the Son of God"—Galatians 2:20), that is, the very faith which governed Jesus Christ now governs me. Paul is not talking of elementary faith in Jesus, but of *the faith which is in the Son of God*, the very faith that was in Jesus is in me, he says.

(b) The New Manners

"Let this mind be in you which was also in Christ Jesus" (Philippians 2:5). There is only one kind of holiness, and that is the holiness of the Lord Jesus. There is only one kind of human nature, and that is the human nature of us all, and Jesus Christ by means of His identification with our human nature can give us the disposition that He had. We have to see to it that we habitually work out that disposition through our eyes and ears and tongues, through all the organs of our bodies and in every detail of our lives.

The apostle Paul has been identified with the death of Jesus Christ, his whole life has been invaded by a new spirit, "by one Spirit we were all baptized into one body" (1 Corinthians 12:13), and now he has no longer any connection with the body of sin, that mystical body which ultimately ends with the devil. We are made part of the mystical Body of Christ by sanctification. We have used the term *invasion* because it gives the idea better than any other.

The illustration our Lord uses of the vine and the branches in John 15 is the most satisfactory one, because it indicates that every bit of the life in the branch which bears fruit is the result of an invasion from the parent stem: "I am the vine, you are the branches" (John 15:5). Our lives are drawn from the Lord Jesus, not only the spring and the motive of life, but our actual thinking and living and doing. This is what Paul means when he talks about the new man in Christ Jesus (see Ephesians 2:15). After sanctification that is where the life is drawn from.

"All my springs are in you" (Psalm 87:7). Notice how God will wither up every other spring you have. He will wither up your natural virtues, He will break up confidence in your natural powers. He will wither up your confidence in brain and spirit and body, until you learn by practical experience that you have no right to draw your life from any source other than the tremendous reservoir of the resurrection life of Jesus Christ.

Thank God if you are going through a drying-up experience! Our Lord never patches up our natural virtues, He replaces the whole person from within, until the new man is shown in the new manners. God does not give new manners; we make our own, but we have to make them out of the new life (Ephesians 4:22–32). Every detail of our physical lives is to be absolutely under the control of the new disposition which God planted in us by means of identification with Jesus Christ, and we shall no longer be allowed to murmur "can't." There is no such a word as *can't* in a Christian's vocabulary if he or she is rightly related to God; there is only one word and that is I *can*.

"I know how to be abased, and I know how to abound. Everywhere and in all things have I learned both to be full and to be hungry, both to abound and to suffer need. I can do all things through Christ who strengthens me" (Philippians 4:12–13). And watch the kind of things Paul said he could do. Manners refer to Christian character, and we are responsible for our manners. God works the alteration within us now, says Paul, "Work out what God works in," and we shall find when we are right with Him that God uses the machinery of our circumstances to enable us to do it.

(c) The New Mankind

God is not after satisfying us and glorifying us; He wants to manifest in us what His Son can do. "When He comes . . . to be glorified in His saints and to be admired among all those who believe" (2 Thessalonians 1:10). The invasion of the life of Jesus Christ makes us sons and daughters of God. These are things that the angels desire to look into. It is as if they look down on us and say, "Look at that woman, how wonderfully like Jesus Christ she is; she used not to be, but look at her now. We know Jesus Christ did it, but we wonder how?" Or, "Look at that man, he is just like his Master, how did Jesus Christ do it?" Thank God we are not going to be angels, we are going to be something tenfold better. By the redemption of Jesus Christ there is a time coming when our bodies will be in the image of God. "Our lowly body" is to be conformed to "His glorious body" (Philippians 3:21) and our bodies will bear the image of God as our spirits do.

5

SOUL: THE ESSENCE, EXISTENCE, AND EXPRESSION

1. **The Term** *Soul*—**Generally**[1]
   (a) Applied to Men and Animals—Genesis 1:20–21, 24, 30
   (b) Applied to Men, Not Animals—Genesis 2:7;
       1 Corinthians 15:45
   (c) Applied to Men Individually—Genesis 12:13; 1 Samuel 18:1
2. **The Truth about the Soul—Specifically**[2]
   (a) And Spirit—Genesis 2:7
   (b) And Body—James 2:26
   (c) And Personality—Isaiah 29:24; Romans 8:16

---

1. N.B.: Never applied to angels or to God (see 2 Corinthians 4:7). Never applied to plants (see Job 14:8–9).
2. N.B.: The spirit is the essential foundation of man; the soul his peculiar essential form; the body his essential manifestation.

We take first of all the term *soul* generally and specifically. The next chapter deals with the fundamental powers of the soul, which means the soul as it is influenced either by a degenerate intelligence or by the Spirit of God; there we shall deal with the varied powers of the soul. Then the fleshly presentation of the soul will be considered, which means the soul manifesting and expressing itself in the bodily life; finally, we shall deal with the past, present and future of the soul, and with the theses that have gathered round the doctrine of the soul, which are quite scriptural and yet lead to conclusions most unscriptural. In the Old Testament the word "soul," meaning the animal soul, the soul that is present only in this order of beings, is mentioned about 460 times. In the New Testament the word "soul" is mentioned about 57 times, with the same meaning. When the Bible mentions a thing over five hundred times, it is time that Christians examined the teaching about it with care.

1. The Term *Soul*

The term *soul* generally, is used in three distinct ways. First, as applied to men and animals alike as distinct from all other creations; second, the more particular use of the word as applied to men distinguished from animals; and third, as applied to one man as distinct from another.

(a) Applied to Men and Animals

The term *soul* here includes animals and people to distinguish them from every other form of creation. The Bible nowhere says that God has a soul; the only way in which the soul of God is referred to is prophetically in anticipation of the Incarnation. Angels are never spoken of as having souls, because soul has reference to this order of creation and angels belong to another order. Our Lord emphatically had a soul, but of God and of angels the term "soul" is not used. The term "soul" is never applied to plants. A plant has life, but the Bible never speaks of it as having soul.

> For there is hope for a tree,
> If it is cut down, that it will sprout again,
> And that its tender shoots will not cease.
> Though its root may grow old in the earth,
> And its stump may die in the ground,
> Yet at the scent of water it will bud
> And bring forth branches like a plant.
> But man dies and is laid away;
> Indeed he breathes his last and where is he?
> (Job 14:7–10)

The distinction there is very clear; you can cut off a piece of a plant and the cut off part will grow; but if you cut off the limb of an animal and plant it, it will not grow, the reason being that a plant has no soul, but an animal has. There is nothing said in the Bible about the immortality of animals. The Bible says that there will be animals in the regenerated earth, but nowhere does it say that the animals which we see now are immortal and that when they die they are raised again. The Bible indicates that everything which partakes of the curse through the Fall will be restored by God's mighty redemption; nothing will be lost.

(b) Applied to Men, Not Animals

"And the LORD God formed man of the dust of the ground, and breathed into his nostrils the breath of life; and man became a living being [soul KJV]" (Genesis 2:7). "And so it is written, 'The first man Adam became a living being [soul].' The last Adam became a life-giving spirit" (1 Corinthians 15:45).

Soul, then, is something peculiar to people and animals, that God has not, that angels have not, and that plants have not.

Human beings have soul, and animals have soul. What kind of spirit does an animal have? Soul is the holder of spirit and body together; then it follows that there must be a spirit in the animal, otherwise we must revise our statement about soul.

There is certainly a spirit in the animal, for the Bible reveals that when an animal dies, its spirit "goes down." The spirit of the animal is part of the spirit of entire nature, and when the animal dies its spirit does back again into entire nature. The spirit of entire nature is manifestly a creation of God. The spirit in the human being which holds his soul and body together is entirely different from the spirit of an animal; it is the human spirit which God created when He breathed into Adam's nostrils the breath of life. God did not make the man a little god; He breathed into his nostrils the spirit which became humanity's distinct spirit, "and man became a living soul."

Where does someone's spirit go when he dies? "Who knows the spirit of the sons of men, which goes upward, and the spirit of the animal, which goes down to the earth?" (Ecclesiastes 3:21). Scientists tell us that death is a molecular disturbance, that when we die we are distributed into the spirit of entire nature. The Bible says that the spirit of man goes back to God. This does not imply that a person's spirit is absorbed into God; but that the human spirit goes back to God with the characteristics on it for either judgment or praise.

When we deal more narrowly with this subject later on, we shall find that the nature of the human spirit, whether it be sensual or spiritual, is to express itself in soul. The whole effort of the spirit is to express itself through the soul, that is, in ordinary physical life.

(c) Applied to Men Individually

"Say, I pray thee, thou art my sister, that it may be well with me for thy sake; and my soul shall live because of thee" (Genesis

12:13 KJV). "Now when he had finished speaking to Saul, the soul of Jonathan was knit to the soul of David, and Jonathan loved him as his own soul" (1 Samuel 18:1). These passages describe the use of the term soul as an individual personal soul distinct from every other soul. An individual soul cannot be divided or cut up. In popular language we speak of a person expressing soul in music, or in literature or art; or we refer to him as being hard and mechanical and *soulless*, and it is to this aspect of soul we are referring here. The phrases *beautiful soul* and *mean soul* refer to the individual aspect of soul.

When demon possession is referred to in the Scripture, (see Luke 8:26–39), the body is the location or habitation of other spirits besides the individual's own spirit. Thought takes up no room, spirit partakes of the nature of thought, and there is no limit to the number of spirits a person's body may hold during demon possession.

2. The Truth about the Soul
(a) The Soul and Spirit

Where did the soul come from? The soul has no existence until the spirit and the body come together; it holds its existence *in fee* entirely by spirit, which statement is the needed complementary truth of what has already been stated, that soul is the holder of spirit and body together.

What is the spirit in a fallen human being? "For what man knows the things of a man except the spirit of the man which is in him? Even so no one knows the things of God except the Spirit of God" (1 Corinthians 2:11). We must approach this subject by making a distinction between the sensual person and the spiritual person. The spirit in a fallen or sensual individual is his mind, which has a vast capacity for God, to whom, however, he is dead, and the spirit of a fallen individual is imprisoned in his soul and degraded by the body.

A sensual person may have marvelous ideas, wonderful intelligence, and yet his whole life may be corrupt and rotten. Take Oscar Wilde, for instance. It would be difficult to find a more flagrant example of gross immorality, and yet while in prison, after a life of unthinkable immorality, Wilde wrote a most amazing book entitled *De Profundis*, a book which shows a wonderful grasp of our Lord's teaching. The spirit in Oscar Wilde was nothing more than an intellectual spirit, a spiritual capacity that had no life in itself and was enslaved by the body through the soul.

Instead of a fallen person's intelligence being able to lift up his body, it does exactly the opposite; a fallen individual's intelligence severs his intellectual life more and more from his bodily life and produces inner hypocrisy. In the case of the lives of certain poets, literary men and women, and geniuses, the exception is to find one who has a clean life as well as a good mind. You can never judge somebody by his intellectual flights. You may hear the most magnificent and inspiring diction from a person who has sunk lower than the beasts in his moral life. He has a sensual spirit; that is, instead of his soul allowing his spirit to lift up his body, it drags it down, and there is a divorce between his intellectual life and his practical life.

A spiritual individual is quite different. Jesus Christ was a spiritual Personality; the Holy Spirit filled His spirit and kept His soul and body in perfect harmony with God. The meaning of the atonement is that Jesus Christ has power to impart to us the Holy Spirit. Holy Spirit has "life in itself," and as soon as that life is manifested in our souls, it wars against what we have been describing. Slowly and surely if we mind the Holy Spirit who fills our spirits and re-energizes them, we shall find that He will lift our souls, and with our souls our bodies, into a totally new unity until the former divorce is annulled. In a spiritual personality the Spirit of Jesus Christ enables the material body of a man or woman to show His nature. The spirit of an individual cannot do this for it has not life in itself.

Never judge anyone by the fact that he has good ideas, and never judge yourself by the fact that you have stirring visions of things. We are told that no one can teach the doctrine of entire sanctification unless he is entirely sanctified himself, but he can. The devil can teach entire sanctification if he pleases. This power is one of the most dangerous powers of the soul. There are spiritual persons and sensual persons. A sensual person is one in whom the divorce between mental conception and practical living is discernible.

The only solution of the problem lies in receiving the Holy Spirit; not believing Him, or complimenting Him, but *receiving* Him. When we receive the Holy Spirit, He so energizes our spirits that we are able to detect the things that are wrong, and we are enabled to rectify them if we mind the Holy Spirit. This is the Scotch use of the term *mind*, and it means "remember to obey." It carries with it the meaning of another Scotch word, *lippen*, that is, "trust." Mind the Holy Spirit, mind His light, mind His convictions, mind His guidance, and slowly and surely the sensual personality will be turned into a spiritual personality.

(b) The Soul and Body

"For as the body without the spirit is dead, so faith without works is dead also" (James 2:26). The body has the earth as its ancestor. "The being of man plants its foot on the earth and the being of earth culminates in man, for both are destined to the fellowship of one history." We have insisted all through these studies that from God's standpoint a person's chief glory is his body. "But we have this treasure in earthen vessels, that the excellence of the power may be of God and not of us" (2 Corinthians 4:7). The "treasure" is God's Spirit being manifested in a human spirit. God's Spirit cannot be manifested in angels, or in animals, or in plants; it can only be manifested in human "earthen vessels."

Do not make that mean that Paul is pouring contempt on the earthen vessel; it is exactly the opposite. Jesus Christ took on Him the nature of the earthen vessel, not the nature of angels. "Of the earth, made of dust" (1 Corinthians 15:47), is humanity's glory, not its shame, and it is in the earth, made of dust, that Jesus Christ's full regenerating work is to have its ultimate reach. The person's body and the earth on which he treads are to partake in the final restitution. Our soul's history is not furthered in spite of our bodies, but because of our bodies.

Nothing can enter the soul but through the senses, God enters into the soul through the senses. "The words that I speak to you are spirit, and they are life" (John 6:63). Beware of the absorption type of mysticism, it is never presented in the Bible. All that the soul retains comes through its bodily senses, and when the Holy Spirit is finding His way into someone's spirit it is through the bodily senses on the physical side. "He shall glorify Me," said Jesus; in my mind, my imagination, in and through my body. And again, He "will bring to your remembrance all things that I said to you" (John 14:26). This can only be done by the material brain working through the body.

Beware of all inward impressions. Beware of all instincts which you cannot curb by the wisdom taught in God's Book. If you take every impression as a call of the Spirit of God, you will end in hallucinations (see 2 Thessalonians 2:10–12). Test every movement by the tests Jesus Christ has given, and they are all tangible, sensible tests. The way to test people, Jesus says, is "by their fruit." We say that the fruit of the Spirit has altogether to do with the spiritual, but the Bible reveals that the spiritual must show itself in the physical. God knows no divorce whatsoever between the three aspects of the human nature, spirit, soul, and body; they must be at one, and they are at one either in damnation or in salvation.

If anyone has not the Holy Spirit of God energizing his spirit, he will come to be judged more and more by the judgment passed on his bodily life. Beware of the people who teach that though someone's body may sin, his soul does not. No such distinctions are taught in God's Word. If a person is not enlivened by the Holy Spirit, his intelligence has no power to lift him; he cannot lift himself by his ideas, or intelligent notions, or knowledge. That is why intelligence is never the primary thing from God's standpoint. "If anyone wills to do His will," says Jesus, "he shall know concerning the doctrine, whether it is from God" (John 7:17)—performance of the will before perception of the doctrine always in spiritual matters.

As soon as we receive the Holy Spirit and are energized by God, we shall find our bodies are the first place of attack for the Enemy, because the body has been the center which ruled the soul and divided it from spiritually intelligent standards; consequently the body is the last stake of Satan. The body is the margin of the battle for you and me. Health is simply the perfect balance of the body with the outer world; when anything upsets that balance we become diseased. As soon as the Holy Spirit comes in, disturbance occurs, physically, morally and spiritually, and the balance is upset. Jesus Christ said, "I did not come to bring peace but a sword" (Matthew 10:34).

What balance will the Holy Spirit give back? The old one? No! We can never get back the old balance of health again; we have to get a new balance, that is, that of holiness, which means the balance of our disposition with God's laws. We shall find the choppy waters come just there. So many misunderstand why it is their bodies are attacked now that they are spiritual in a way they never were attacked before they were spiritual. We shall deal later with the difference between natural sickness and demoniacal sickness. The Bible has a great deal to say about them both. The Bible is the only Book that throws light on our physical condition, on our soul condition, and on our spiritual condition.

In the Bible the sense of smell and sight, and the other senses, are not used as metaphors only; they are identified with the nature of the soul's life. This accounts for what people are apt to call the vulgar teaching of the Bible. God has safeguarded us in every way. Spiritism is the great crime; it pushes down God's barriers and brings us into contact with forces we cannot control. On the other hand, if we give ourselves over to Jesus Christ and are ruled by Him, the Holy Spirit can do through us anything He chooses. "I beseech you, therefore, brethren . . . present your bodies a living sacrifice" (Romans 12:1), and "bodies" means "faculties" as well. Why should we expect God to deal with less than the devil deals with? A good man or woman is a flesh and blood good man or woman, not an impression. The body is the vessel of the soul, and it enables the soul to turn its inward life into an outward life.

6

SOUL: THE ESSENCE, EXISTENCE, AND EXPRESSION

Fundamental Powers of the Soul

1. **Contraction**
   (a) First Power—Self-Comprehending—Deuteronomy 13:6–7; 1 Samuel 18:1
   (b) Second Power—Stretching Beyond Itself—Psalm 27:12
2. **Expansion.**
   (c) Third Power—Self-Living—Job 2:6; John 10:11
   (d) Fourth Power—Spirit-Penetrated—Isaiah 26:9; Jude 19
3. **Rotation.**
   (e) Fifth Power—Stirred Sensually or Spiritually—Exodus 23:9; 1 Peter 2:11
   (f) Sixth Power—Speaking the Spirit's Thoughts—Genesis 41:40
   (g) Seventh Power—Sum Total in Unity—Jeremiah 38:16

1. Contraction

We mean by *fundamental*, the powers that work in the interior of the soul. The soul's existence has its origin in the spirit and in its struggle to realize itself. This is the counterpart of the statement made in the last chapter, that is, that the soul is the holder of the body and spirit together. By *contraction*, we mean that the soul has power to contract into itself. By *expansion*, we mean that soul has power to strive away from itself, reaching beyond itself; and by *rotation* we mean that the soul has the power of expressing itself by the restlessness of becoming.

This mechanical division is merely an arbitrary way of presenting a complex truth. All scientific laws exist in people's heads and are simply attempts to explain observed facts. For instance it is a dangerous mistake to talk about the law of gravity as if it were a thing. The law of gravity is the explanation given by scientific people of certain observed facts, and to say that Jesus Christ "broke the law of gravity" when He walked on the sea, and when He ascended, is a misstatement. He brought in a new series of facts for which the law of gravity, so-called, could not account.

(a) First Power—Self-Comprehending

"If . . . your friend who is as your own soul, secretly entices you, saying, 'Let us go and serve other gods,' which you have not known . . ." (Deuteronomy 13:6–7; see also 1 Samuel 18:1.) These verses indicate the power of the soul to comprehend itself as an individual separate from every other individual. Watch your own experience, and you will recognize this soul power at once. When a child begins to be self-conscious, it is this power that is awakening, the power to contract into itself and to realize that it is different from its father and mother and from all other children, and the tendency to shut up the life to itself increases.

This power shows itself in feelings of isolation and separation, alternating between pride and shyness. Self-consciousness drags down the harmony of the soul. In some people it lasts a long time; some never get beyond the manifestation of this power of soul, that is, the power to contract into themselves, the power to be different from everybody else; they have not gone on to realize that they have the power to expand, that is, to come into contact with other souls without being afraid or timid. That is the first power in a natural soul.

Now take it in a soul born again of the Spirit of God, how does this power of the soul express itself? The power of self-comprehension in a born-again soul shows itself in opposition to sinfulness. Watch the swing of the pendulum, as it were, in your own life, and in the life of anybody newly born again of the Spirit; the life goes to the opposite extreme of the way it lived when in the world—if it was given to finery and dress when in the world, it will go to the opposite extreme on its introduction to the new life. This is the first recognizable power of an individual soul.

(b) Second Power—Stretching Beyond Itself

"Do not deliver me to the will of my adversaries; for false witnesses have risen against me, and such as breathe out violence" (Psalm 27:12). This power of the soul causes a person to find out first not the forces in agreement with it, but those that are different from it. Other souls seem to be in opposition to it. The boy who has become self-conscious always imagines every other boy is his enemy, and he suspects any boy who wants to become his friend. This power of the soul also makes a person realize that he can do pretty well what he likes with his body—a dangerous moment in a human life. Or again it makes a person realize he is able to deceive everyone else.

There is no restriction at all when this power first dawns. I realize I can satisfy my bodily appetites as I choose; I can also cunningly deceive everyone else. If I am a servant, I can easily defraud my master or mistress; if I am a businessperson, I can defraud the public. This power of the soul can be seen worked out to its complete issue in the life of the world.

In a spiritual nature this power of the soul shows itself in opposition to sinful craving. Jesus Christ says, in effect: "If you are My disciple, you will easily be defrauded, but you will not allow yourself to be defrauded from the simplicity of the gospel." Knowledge of evil broadens a person's mind, makes him tolerant, but paralyses his action. Knowledge of good broadens a person's mind, makes him intolerant of all sin, and shows itself in intense activity. A bad person, an evil-minded individual, is amazingly tolerant of everything and everyone, no matter whether they are good or bad, Christian or not, but his power of action is paralyzed entirely. He is tolerant of everything—the devil, the flesh, the world, sin, and everything else.

Jesus Christ never tolerated sin for one moment, and when His nature is getting its way in a soul the same intolerance is shown, and it manifests itself "not with eyeservice" (Ephesians 6:6). If I am a servant I won't serve my master or mistress with this power of my soul realizing I have power to deceive. I will use it to show that I belong to Jesus Christ. Neither shall I use this power of my soul to do what I like with my body. "Not with eyeservice, as men-pleasers, but as bondservants of Christ, doing the will of God from the heart" (Ephesians 6:6). "Bondservants, obey in all things your masters according to the flesh, not with eyeservice as men-pleasers, but in sincerity of heart, fearing God" (Colossians 3:22). In a spiritual soul this power of the soul will show itself in intense opposition to all sinful cravings. A soul that is born again does everything, from sweeping a room to preaching the gospel, from cleaning streets to governing a nation, for the glory of God. This second power of the soul enables it to stretch beyond itself; the whole mainspring of the soul's life is altered.

2. Expansion

(c) Third Power—Self-Living

"I am the good shepherd: the good shepherd gives His life for the sheep" (John 10:11). "And the LORD said to Satan, 'Behold, he is in your hand, but spare his life'" (Job 2:6). These passages refer to the one power in a person that neither God nor the devil can touch without the person's sanction. The devil has power up to a certain point, but he cannot touch someone's life, and whenever Jesus Christ presents the gospel of God to a soul, it is always on the line of "Are you willing?" There is never any coercion. God has so constituted us that there must be a free willingness on our part.

This power is at once the most fearful and the most glorious power. A human soul can withstand the devil successfully, and it can also withstand God successfully. This self-living power is the essence of the human spirit, which is as immortal as God's Spirit and as indestructible; whether the human spirit be good or bad, it is as immortal as God. This power of the soul enables it to put itself on a par with God; this is the very essence of Satan. The power that can make someone either a peer of the Lord or a peer of the devil is the most terrible power of the soul. Jesus Christ is referring to this power when He says, "I lay down My life of Myself; no man takes it from Me" (John 10:17–18).

When the soul is born again and lifted into the domain our Lord lives in, this power shows itself in opposition to sinful passionateness. *Passionateness* means something that carries everything before it. The prince of this world is intense, and the Spirit of God is intense. When Paul talks about the flesh and the Spirit working in a person's soul, he expresses the intensity by using the word *lust*. The Spirit lusts—passionately desires—the whole life for God; and the mind of the flesh lusts—passionately longs for—the whole life back again in the service of the world.

In the spiritual realm passionateness also means something that overcomes every obstacle. When the writer to the Hebrews talks about perfection, he means this overwhelming passion which carries a soul right on to all God has for it. "Be filled with the Spirit" (Ephesians 5:18), this is the key word of life. The Bible indicates that we overcome the world not by passionlessness, not by the patience of exhaustion, but by passion, the passion of an intense and all-consuming love for God. This is the characteristic in a born-again soul—opposition to every sinful passionateness. Do insist in your own mind that God does not work in vague, gentle impressions in a human soul, but in violent oppositions which rend and tear the soul, making it, instead of a place of harmonious happiness, exactly the opposite for a season. This experience is true in every soul that is going on with God. When we are first introduced to the life of God there is violent opposition to everything that used to be prevalent, and that it is so is not a mistake, it is what God intends, because there is the force of a totally new life.

(d) Fourth Power—Spirit-Penetrated

"With my soul have I desired You in the night—yes, by my spirit within me will I seek You early" (Isaiah 26:9; see also Jude 19). We mean by spirit-penetrated the spiritual power in the human which struggles to express itself in soul. The spirit of the human in an unregenerate nature is the power of mind not energized by the Holy Spirit which has no "life in itself." It proves utterly futile in lifting the body, and produces a great divorce between the ideal and the real.

Every kind of intellectual excellence is a snare of Satan unless the spirit of the individual has been renewed by the incoming of the Spirit of God. A person's intellect may give him noble ideas and power to express them through his soul in language but it does not give him power to carry them into action. The charge of idolatry is very apt here.

We are apt to ridicule, or pass over with a smile, the descriptions given of idolatry in, say, the book of Isaiah, where the writer refers to a tree being taken and one part of it used to cook the person's food and the other part is carved into an idol before which he bows and worships; yet this is exactly what people do with their ideas.

The intellect forms ideas for guiding a person's physical life, and then takes other ideas and worships them as God, and if someone has made his own ideas his god he is greater than his own god. This is not such a terrible power, perhaps, as the self-living power of the soul, but it is a power that will work havoc unless the soul is right with God. It is the power that produces internal hypocrisy, the power that makes me able to think good thoughts while I live a bad life, unconvicted.

How does this power show itself in those who are born again of the Spirit of God? This power shows itself in opposition to secularity. Take your own experience, those of you who are spiritual—spiritual in the biblical sense, identified with the Lord Jesus Christ in a practical way—you cannot make a distinction now between secular and sacred, it is all sacred; but in the first realization of this power the line is drawn clearly and strongly between what is called secular and what is called sacred. In the life of Jesus Christ there was no division into secular and sacred, but with us when this power begins to be realized it always manifests itself in a line of cleavage. There are certain things we won't do, certain things we won't look at, certain things we won't eat, certain hours we won't sleep. It is not wrong; it is the Spirit of God in a soul beginning to utilize the powers of the soul for God; and as the soul goes on it comes to a full-orbed condition, where it manifests itself as in the life of the Lord Jesus and all is sacred.

If you obey the Spirit of God and practice in your physical life all that God has put in your heart by His Spirit, when the crisis comes you will find your nature will stand by you. So many people misunderstand why they fall. It comes from this idea, "Now I have received the grace of God, I am all right." Paul says he did not "frustrate the grace of God," that is, receive it in vain. If we do not go on practicing day by day and week by week, working out what God has worked in, when a crisis comes God's grace is there right enough, but our natures are not. Our natures have not been brought into line by practice and consequently do not stand by us, and down we go and then we blame God. We must bring out bodily lives into line by practice day by day, hour by hour, moment by moment, then when the crisis comes we shall find not only God's grace but our own natures will stand by us, and the crisis will pass without any disaster at all. Exactly the opposite will happen—the soul will be built up into a stronger attitude toward God.

3. Rotation

(e) Fifth Power—Stirred Sensually or Spiritually

"Also you shall not oppress a stranger, for you know the heart of a stranger, because you were strangers in the land of Egypt" (Exodus 23:9). "Beloved, I beg you as sojourners and pilgrims, abstain from fleshly lusts which war against the soul" (1 Peter 2:11). Remember that the soul is manifested as the spirit struggles to make itself expressed. Exodus 23:19 is a magnificent passage; it is intensely, movingly practical in every detail, and there this power of the soul is clearly recognizable. It fits itself on with the second power, that is, the power we have to deceive everybody else, to do cunning things, to defraud, to utilize other people for our own ends; and the warning is, be careful not to be stirred in your soul by the wrong spirit. If the soul can be stirred by its own cunning, the cunning of one's own inner nature, it can be stirred by vileness and abominable sensuality through the senses (1 Peter 2:11).

How does this power show itself in a regenerate soul? It shows itself in opposition to worldly bondage. You will find in your own experience, and in all recorded experiences, that when the life is going on along God's line, God puts the fear of you on those who are on the outside because of the scorn you have of worldly bondages. The Spirit of God in you will not allow you to bow your neck to any yoke but the yoke of the Lord Jesus Christ. When you stand on this platform of God's grace, you see instantly that the bondage is in the world. The etiquette and standards of the world are an absolute bondage, and those who live in them are abject slaves, and yet the extraordinary thing is that when a worldly person sees anyone emancipated and under the yoke of the Lord Jesus Christ, he says they are in bondage, whereas exactly the opposite is true. True liberty exists only when the soul has this holy scorn in it, "I will bow my neck to no yoke but the yoke of the Lord Jesus Christ." Our Lord was meek to all that His Father did, but intolerant to all the devil did; He would not suffer compromise with the devil in any shape or form. This power of the soul, then, when the soul is born again, manifests itself in opposition to all worldly bondage.

(f) Sixth Power—Speaking the Spirit's Thoughts

"You shall be over my house, and all my people shall be ruled according to your word; only in regard to the throne will I be greater than you" (Genesis 41:40). We are now dealing with rotation, the restlessness of becoming. That is how all these powers are going to manifest themselves in a fully matured soul. Genesis 41:40 is a picture of a soul right with God; but remember there is a corresponding picture. Anyone in whom all the powers of the soul are developing will come to a place where he shows literally, not only with his mouth, but with his eyes and every power of his body, who is on the throne of his life. If it is the prince of this world, the individual is prime minister of his own body under the devil. When the full powers of the soul are developed I am obliged to carry out the wishes of the ruling monarch.

How does this power show itself when a soul is born again of the Spirit of God? It shows itself in opposition to worldly thoughts and customs. "Only in regard to the throne will I be greater than you." Take Pharaoh as a picture of Jesus Christ; the soul that is born again and is going on with God, who has been identified with Jesus Christ in practical sanctification and has the full powers of the soul developed and manifested, that soul is prime minster of his own body under Jesus Christ's domin- ion. That is the ideal, and it is not an ideal only, but an ideal which Jesus Christ expects us to carry out—all the powers of the soul working through the body in an express personality, revealing the Ruler to be the Lord Jesus Christ.

(g) Seventh Power—Sum Total in Unity

"As the LORD lives, who made our very souls, I will not put you to death, nor will I give you into the hand of these men who seek your life" (Jeremiah 38:16). The sum total is a perfect unity of badness or a perfect unity of goodness. "All the souls that came with Jacob into Egypt" (Genesis 46:26 KJV). The word *soul* there refers to the full maturity of the powers mani- fested in the bodily life. This is the description of a full-grown individual, whether he is bad or good, and when a soul gets into full maturity of expression, the chances are he will never alter. In Jeremiah 38:16, soul is mentioned in the same way. This is not the soul in its beginnings, in its chaotic state, but the soul absolutely mastered by the ruling spirit and expressing itself through the body.

How does this perfection of soul life show itself in a born-again person who is living the life God wants him to live? It shows itself in opposition to all other powers, and manifests itself in its bodily life in "the wisdom that is from above" (James 3:17). It is literally the uncrushable loveliness of a soul manifesting God's rule, all its powers now in harmony. This is not in heaven, but on earth. It is not mental perfection, nor bodily perfection; it is the perfection of a soul's attitude when all its powers are under the control of the Spirit of God. All the corners have been chipped away; all the extreme swinging of the pendulum has been regulated; all the chaotic turmoil has become ordered, and the life is now manifesting the life of the Lord Jesus in its mortal flesh (see 2 Corinthians 4:11).

By way of revision, we find that these powers of the soul show themselves in every one of us more or less. For instance, we would never think of judging a boy or girl by the same standard of judgment we would pass on them when they are mature, because a boy or a girl is not in full grip of a character; but when a soul is matured, the character which is manifested meets with severe judgment. There is no excuse to be made for it now; all its powers are consolidated and the wrong it does is not the wrong of an impulse, it is the wrong of a dead set.

When the soul is consolidated and is right with God, the whole character manifests something which bears a strong family likeness to Jesus Christ. There is, however, a chaotic period in Christian experience. Read the apostle Paul's earnest, almost motherlike, solicitation over his young converts; he almost seems to *croon* over them, to use an old Scotch word, to agonize in heart over them, because of the chaotic state of their souls. Jesus Christ commissioned Peter, and the other disciples through him to "feed My lambs."

7

SOUL: THE ESSENCE, EXISTENCE, AND EXPRESSION

Fleshly Presentation of the Soul

1. In Embryo
   (a) Before Consciousness—Psalm 139:15; Hosea 12:3;
       Genesis 25:22; Luke 1:41
   (b) Breath Consciousness—Genesis 2:7; Isaiah 2:22
   (c) Blood Circulation—Genesis 9:4; Leviticus 17:10, 14
2. In Evolution
   (a) Hub of Life—Proverbs 4:23
   (b) Hubbub of Life
      (1) Sense of Sight—Psalm 119:37
      (2) Sense of Hearing—Job 12:11
      (3) Sense of Taste—Psalm 119:103
      (4) Sense of Smell—Genesis 8:21; 2 Corinthians 2:14–16
      (5) Sense of Touch—Acts 17:27; 1 John 1:1

3. In Expression
   (a) Hilarity of Life—Ecclesiastes 11:9; Luke 6:45
   (b) Himself—Judges 8:18; Luke 2:40, 52; Ephesians 4:13

By the word *fleshly* we do not mean what the apostle Paul meant when he uses the word in his epistles; we are using the word to denote this natural body. Paul's use of the word, unless prefaced with *mortal*, means a disposition of mind. The subject is divided under three headings: In Embryo, In Evolution, and In Expression. *Embryo* means in the beginning; *Evolution* means growth, the growth of the human soul. Evolution is a fact both scientific and scriptural, that is, if we mean by *evolution* that there is growth in every species, but not growth from one species into another. There is growth in a plant, in an animal and in a human, and that is the only way in which we use the word. The last division simply means the *Expression* of the soul in and through the body.

1. In Embryo

(a) Before Consciousness

   "And it happened, when Elizabeth heard the greeting of Mary, that the babe leaped in her womb; and Elizabeth was filled with the Holy Spirit" (Luke 1:41; see also Genesis 25:22; Hosea 12:3). In the very beginning of human life, body, soul and spirit are together. "My frame was not hidden from You, when I was made in secret, and skillfully wrought in the lowest parts of the earth" (Psalm 139:15). Modern tendencies of thought which are working great havoc indicate that a child has not a soul until it is born into this world. The Bible says that body, soul, and spirit develop together. This may not appear to the majority of us as being of any importance, but it will do so when we come in contact with the views that are abroad today, even among some who call themselves Christian teachers, but who are really wolves among the sheep and whose teaching comes from the bottomless pit.

(b) Breath Consciousness

"And the LORD God formed man of the dust of the ground, and breathed into his nostrils the breath of life; and man became a living soul" (Genesis 2:7 KJV; see also Isaiah 2:22). In a multitude of verses in the Bible, the soul life and the breath of the body are identified. The Bible teaches that it is not the body that breathes, but the soul. The body did not breathe in the beginning before God breathed into Adam's nostrils the breath of life; so as far as conscious soul life is concerned, it depends on our breathing. All through God's Book the soul life is connected with the breathing; in fact, it is incorporated into our idea of life that when breath is suspended, life is gone. "The soul is departed" is the popular phrase.

(c) Blood Circulation

"But you shall not eat flesh with its life, that is, its blood" (Genesis 9:4; see also Leviticus 17:10–14). In the Bible the soul is connected and identified with breath and blood—two fleshly, physical things. In Genesis 9:4 blood and soul are alternate terms, they are identified completely, and the verses in God's Book that prove this are innumerable. When the blood is spilt, the soul is gone; when the breath is taken, the soul is gone. The whole life of a person consists physically in his breath and in his blood. The soul in working itself into the blood never fails to impart to it the peculiar character of its own life. This psychologically is brought out very clearly by our Lord's statement in John 6:53, "Unless you eat the flesh of the Son of Man, and drink His blood, you have no life in you."

An unobvious revelation is that when I eat and drink and discern the Lord's body, or, in other words, receive my food and drink from Him, the physical nourishment thus derived enables my Lord to manifest Himself in my flesh and blood. If I do not discern the Lord's body, and do not receive my food from Him, my physical nourishment will humiliate Him in me.

The ruling disposition of the soul shows itself in the blood, the physical blood. In every language, good blood and bad blood is referred to; merciful blood and tender blood, hot or cold blood, and this is based on Scriptural teaching. Jesus Christ insists on the fact that if we are His disciples it will be revealed in the blood, meaning, the physical life. The old soul tyranny and disposition, the old selfish determination to seek our own ends manifests itself in our bodies, through our blood; and when that disposition of soul is altered, the alteration shows itself at once in the blood also. Instead of the old tempers and the old passions being manifested in our physical blood, the good temper reveals itself. It never does to remove Jesus Christ's spiritual teaching into the domain of the inane and vague—it must come right down where the devil works; and just as the devil works not in vague ways but through flesh and blood, so does the Lord, and the characteristics of the soul for better or worse are shown in the blood.

The first fundamental reference in the verse, "And without shedding of blood is no remission" (Hebrews 9:22), is unquestionably to our Lord's atonement; and yet there is a direct reference to us. Do we begin to know what the Bible means by "the blood of Jesus Christ"? Blood and life are inseparable. In the Bible the experiences of salvation and sanctification are never separated as we separate them; they are separable in experience, but when God's Book speaks of being "in Christ" it is always in terms of entire sanctification.

We are apt to look upon the blood of Christ as a kind of

magic-working thing, instead of an impartation of His very life. The whole purpose of being born again and being identified with the death of the Lord Jesus is that His blood may flow through our mortal bodies; then the tempers and the affections and the dispositions which we manifested in the life of the Lord will be manifested in us in some degree. Present-day wise talk pushes all the teaching of Jesus Christ into a remote domain, but the New Testament drives its teaching straight down to the essential necessity of the physical expression of spiritual life; that just as the bad soul life shows itself in the body, so the good soul life will show itself there too.

There are two sides to the atonement—it is not only the life of Christ *for* me but His life *in* me for my life; no Christ *for* me if I do not have Christ *in* me. All through there is to be this strenuous, glorious practicing in our bodily lives of the changes which God has worked out in our souls through His Spirit, and the only proof that we are in earnest is that we work out what God works in. As we apply this truth to ourselves, we shall find in practical experience that God does alter passions and nerves and tempers. God alters every physical thing in a human being so that these bodies can be used now as slaves to the new disposition. We can make our eyes, and ears, and every one of our bodily organs express as slaves the altered disposition of our souls.

Remember, then, that blood is the manifestation of the soul life, and that all through the Bible God applies moral characteristics to the blood. The expressions "innocent blood" and "guilty blood" have reference to the soul, and the soul life must show itself in the physical connection.

2. In Evolution

(a) Hub of Life

"Keep your heart with all diligence, for out of it spring the issues of life" (Proverbs 4:23). *Hub* literally means the center of a wheel, and the word is used here to indicate the center of the soul life, of the personal life and the spirit life. This will be dealt with more fully when we come to the chapters on *heart*. The Bible places in the heart everything that the modern psychologist places in the head.

(b) Hubbub of Life

By *hubbub* we mean exactly what the word implies, a tremendous confusion. The confusion in the soul life is brought about by the exercise of our senses. "In the Bible, psychological terms are not merely metaphors, but reflect the organic condition of the soul." The body makes itself inward by means of the soul, and the spirit makes itself outward by means of the soul. The soul is the binder of these two together. There is not one part of the human body left out in God's Book; every part is dealt with and made to have a direct connection either with sin or with holiness. It is not accidental but part of the Divine revelation.

The five senses do not seem to the majority of us to have any spiritual meaning, but in the Bible they have. In the Bible the senses are dealt with in anything but a slight manner; they are dealt with as being expressions of the soul life. The Bible reveals that every part of human physical life is closely connected with sin or with salvation, and that anything that sin has put wrong, Jesus Christ can put right. We are dealing with soul as it expresses itself though the body. The organs of the body are used as indicators of the state of the spiritual life. We mentioned previously in connection with breathing that the internal part of someone's being is affected by his spiritual relationships. If his spiritual connections are not right with God, his bodily condition will, sooner or later, manifest the disorganization. This is proved over and over again in the case of mental diseases. In most insane persons a bodily organ is seriously affected, and the old method of dealing with insanity was to try and get that organ healed. The modern method is simply to leave the organ alone and concentrate on the brain. When the mind is right, the disease in the organ disappears.

(1) Sense of Sight

"Turn away my eyes from looking at worthless things, and revive me in Your way" (Psalm 119:37). How am I going to have my eyes kept from beholding worthless things? By having the disposition of my soul altered. God controls the whole thing, and you will find that you can control it too when He has given you a start. That is the marvelous impetus of the salvation of Jesus Christ. Our eyes record to the brain what they look at, but our disposition makes our eyes look at what it wants them to look at, and they will soon pay no attention to anything else. When the disposition is right, the eyes, literally the body, may be placed wherever you like and the disposition will guard what it records. This is not a figure of speech; it is a literal experience. God does alter the desire to look at the things we used to look at, and we find our eyes are guarded because He has altered the disposition of the soul's life.

(2) Sense of Hearing

"Does not the ear test words?" (Job 12:11). Jesus Christ continually referred to hearing: "He who has ears to hear, let him hear!" (Matthew 11:15). We say that He means the ears of our hearts, but that is very misleading. He means our physical ears which are trained to hear by the disposition of the soul life. God spoke to Jesus once and the people said it thundered, Jesus did not think it thundered; His ears were trained by the disposition of His soul to know His Father's voice (See John 12:28–30). We can elaborate this thought endlessly all through God's Book. I will always hear what I listen for, and the ruling disposition of the soul determines what I listen for, just as the ruling disposition either keeps the eyes from beholding worthless things or makes them behold nothing else.

When Jesus Christ alters our dispositions He gives us the power to hear as He hears. A telegraph operator does not hear the ticking of the machine, his ears are trained to detect the message; we detect only the jingle and tapping of the machine and can make nothing of it. You hear people say, "Thank God, I heard His voice!" How did they hear it? The disposition of the soul enabled the ears to hear something which the soul interpreted at once. It is always true that we only hear what we want to hear, and we shout the other sounds down by controversy and dispute.

"Who has believed our *report*?" literally, "that which we have heard"; "and to whom has the arm of the LORD been revealed?" (Isaiah 53:1). We have either a disposition of soul that can discern the arm of the Lord, or we are just like the beasts of the field who take things as they come and see nothing in them. "I was like a beast before You" (Psalm 73:22), said the psalmist, that is, without any spiritual intelligence. The disposition of my soul determines what I see, and the disposition of my soul determines what I hear.

(3) Sense of Tasting

"How sweet are Your words to my taste, sweeter than honey to my mouth!" (Psalm 119:103). We are getting more and more remote and more difficult to understand from the ordinary, unspiritual standpoint. We have entirely divorced tasting and smelling, seeing and hearing and touching, from spiritual conditions, because the majority of Christian workers have never been trained in what the Bible has to say about us. It can be proved over and over again not only in personal experience, but all through God's Book, that He does alter the taste, not merely mental tastes, but physical tastes, the taste for food and drink; but there is something far more practical even than that, the blessing of God on our soul life gives us an added sensitivity of soul akin to taste or to sight or hearing.

(4) Sense of Smell

"The LORD smelled a soothing aroma. Then the LORD said in His heart, 'I will never again curse the ground for man's sake'" (Genesis 8:21; see also 2 Corinthians 2:14–16). The Bible has a great deal to say about the sense of smell, and yet it is the one sense we make nothing of. This sense to the majority of us has only one meaning, that is, an olfactory nerve that makes us conscious of pleasant things or of exactly the opposite; but the Bible deals with the sense of smell in another way.

Read the following quotation from a book written by Helen Keller, entitled *The World I Live In*; the chapter is entitled, "Smell, the Fallen Angel." Remember, Helen Keller writes as one who can neither see nor hear.

> For some inexplicable reason the sense of smell does not hold the high position it deserves among its sisters. There is something of the fallen angel about it. When it woos us with woodland scents and beguiles us with the fragrance of lovely gardens, it is admitted frankly to our discourse. But when it gives us warning of something noxious in our vicinity, it is treated as if the demon had the upper hand of the angel, and is relegated to outer darkness, punished for its faithful service. It is most difficult to keep the true significance of words when one discusses the prejudices of mankind and I find it hard to give an account of odor perceptions which shall at once be dignified and truthful.
>
> In my experience, smell is most important, and I find that there is high authority for the nobility of the sense which we have neglected and disparaged. It is

recorded that the Lord commanded that incense be burnt before Him continually with a sweet savor. I doubt if there is any sensation arising from sight more delightful than the odors which filter through sun-warmed, wind-tossed branches, or the tide of scents which swells, subsides, and rises again wave on wave, filling the wide world with invisible sweetness.

A whiff of the universe makes us dream of worlds we have never seen, recalls in a flash entire epochs of our dearest experiences. I never smell daisies without living over again the ecstatic mornings that my teacher and I spent wandering in the fields while I learned new words and the names of things. Smell is a potent wizard that transports us across a thousand miles and all the years we have lived. The odor of fruits wafts me to my Southern home, to my childish frolics in the peach orchard. Other odors, instantaneous and fleeting, cause my heart to dilate joyously or contract with remembered grief. Even as I think of smells, my nose is full of scents that start awake sweet memories of summers gone and ripening grain-fields far away.

In Helen Keller the sense of smell takes the place of sight. This is a case which brings the Bible idea more home to us. Let this subject be revised in our Bible study, and let us see whether we are not treating whole tracts of our sense-life indifferently, not understanding that we can develop and cultivate eyes and nose and mouth and ears and every organ of the body to manifest the disposition which Jesus Christ has put into us. Every sense that has been disorganized can be reorganized; not only the senses that we are dealing with, but other senses, every one of them is mentioned in God's Book and is regulated either by the Spirit of God or by the spirit of Satan.

When Paul refers to lust he never places it in the body, but in the disposition of the soul. "Therefore do not let sin reign in your mortal body, that you should obey its lusts" (Romans 6:12). Jesus Christ had a fleshly body as we have, but He was never tempted by lust, because lust resides in the ruling disposition, not in the body. When God changes the ruling disposition, the same body that was used as the instrument of sin to work all manner of uncleanness and unrighteousness can now be used as the slave of the new disposition. It is not a different body; it is the same body with a new disposition.

(5) Sense of Touch

"That they should seek the Lord, in the hope that they might grope for Him and find Him, though He is not far from each one of us" (Acts 17:27). "That which . . . our hands have handled, concerning the Word of life" (1 John 1:1). These passages refer not to mental feeling, but to real, downright, bodily feeling. The disciples had felt God incarnate in Jesus Christ. This is where the issue is so strong between New Testament teaching and the Unitarian teaching. God does not ignore feeling and the sense of touch; He elevates them. The first effort of the soul toward bringing the body into harmony with the new disposition is an effort of faith. The soul has not yet got the body under way, therefore in the meanwhile feeling has to be discounted. When the new disposition enters the soul, the first steps have to be taken in the dark, without feeling; but as soon as the soul has gained control, all bodily organs are brought into physical harmony with the ruling disposition.

3. In Expression

(a) Hilarity of Life

Rejoice, O young man, in your youth,
And let your heart cheer you in the days of your youth;

Walk in the ways of your heart,
And in the sight of your eyes;
But know that for all these
God will bring you into judgment.

(Ecclesiastes 11:9)

"For out of the abundance of the heart his mouth speaks" (Luke 6:45). These passages refer to the physical hilarity of life. Remember, a bad man whose life is wrong has a hilariously happy time, and a good man whose life is right has a hilarious time. All in between are more or less diseased and sick, there is something wrong somewhere: the healthy pagan and the healthy saint are the only ones who are hilarious.

The New Testament writers, especially the apostle Paul, are intense on the hilarity of life. Enthusiasm is the idea, intoxicated with the life of God. Watch nature—if people do not get thrilled in the right way, they will get thrilled in the wrong way. If they are not thrilled by the Spirit of God they will try to get thrilled with strong drink. "Do not be drunk with wine, in which is dissipation" (Ephesians 5:18), says Paul, "but be filled with the Spirit." We have no business to be half-dead spiritually, to hang like clogs on God's plan; we have no business to be sickly, unless it is a preparatory stage for something better, or God is nursing us through some spiritual illness; but if it is the main characteristic of the life, there is something wrong somewhere.

Psalm 73 describes the bad man as having "more than heart could wish" (73.7); this is the expression of soul satisfaction without God. When Solomon says that to fear the Lord shall be "strength to your bones" (Proverbs 3:8), he is talking about the physical bones which are affected amazingly by the condition of the soul life.

In Luke 11, our Lord gives a description of the bad man:

"When a strong man, fully armed, guards his own palace, his goods are in peace," meaning, when Satan, the prince of this world, guards this world, his goods—the souls of people—are in peace; they are quite happy, hilarious, and full of life. One of the most misleading statements is that worldlings have not a happy time; they have a thoroughly happy time.

The point is that their happiness is on the wrong level, and when they come across Jesus Christ, who is the enemy of all that happiness, they experience annoyance. People must be persuaded that Jesus Christ has a higher type of life for them, otherwise they feel they had better not have come across Him. When a worldly person who is happy, moral, and upright comes in contact with Jesus Christ, who came to destroy all that happiness and peace and put it on a different level, he or she has to be persuaded that Jesus Christ is a Being worthy to do this, and instead of the gospel being attractive at first, it is the opposite. When the gospel is presented to an unsaved, healthy, happy, hilarious person, there is violent opposition straight away.

The gospel of Jesus Christ does not present what people want, it presents exactly what they need. As long as you talk about being happy and peaceful, people like to listen to you; but talk about having the disposition of the soul altered, and that the garden of the soul has first of all to be turned into a wilderness and afterwards into a garden of the Lord, and you will find opposition right away.

(b) Himself

We mean by "himself," not God, but man. "Till we all come to the unity of the faith and of the knowledge of the Son of God, to a perfect man, to the measure of the stature of the fullness of Christ" (Ephesians 4:13; see also Judges 8:18; Luke 2:40, 52). In these passages we have a description splendidly given of a full-orbed man. A full-orbed bad man or woman (bad in God's sight) is a wonderful being to look at and a full-orbed man or woman who is right with God is also a wonderful being to look at. The rest of us are simply beings in the making. There is a tremendous fascination about a completely bad man; there is nothing more desirable from the standpoint of this world than a thoroughly well-trained bad man or woman, but he or she is the opponent of Jesus Christ and hate Him with every power of the soul; I mean the Jesus Christ of the New Testament.

God grant that the ruling disposition of our souls may be so altered that we work out the alteration practically. If we have come into experiential touch with the grace of God and have received His Spirit, are we working it out? Is every organ of our bodies enslaved to the new disposition? Or are we using our eyes for what we want to see, and our bodies for our right to ourselves? If so, we have received the grace of God in vain. God grant that we may determine to work out through our bodies the life which Jesus Christ has put into us by His Spirit.

8

SOUL: THE ESSENCE, EXISTENCE, AND EXPRESSION

Past, Present, and Future of the Soul

1. Pre-existence[1]

    (a) Spurious Speculations—Deuteronomy 29:29; Revelation 5:3

    (b) Startling Scriptures—Jeremiah 1:5; Malachi 3:1; Romans 9:11, 13; Luke 1:41

    (c) Steadying Scriptures

        (1) No Soul before Body—Genesis 1–2

        (2) No Soul Destiny Pre-Adamic—Romans 5:12

        (3) No Soul but by Procreation—Genesis 5

    (d) The Pre-existence of Our Lord

---

1. N.B.: Note the pre-existence of our Lord Jesus Christ (John 17:5).

84

2. Present Existence
    (a) Satisfaction of the Soul—Psalm 66:9, 12, 16; Isaiah 55:3
    (b) Sins and Surroundings of the Soul—Proverbs 18:7;
        Psalm 6; Ezekiel 18:4; 1 Peter 1:9
    (c) Supernatural Setting for the Soul—Luke 9:54–56;
        Ephesians 6:12; 1 Corinthians 10:20–21[2]

3. Perpetual Existence
    (a) Mortal Aspect of the Soul—Job 14:2; James 4:14
    (b) Immortal Aspect of the Soul—Luke 16:19, 31; 23:43
    (c) Eternal Life and Eternal Death of the Soul—Matthew
        10:28; Romans 5:21; 6:23

In concluding our general survey of this great theme of the Soul, we purpose to sketch in outline the past, present, and future states of the soul.

1. Pre-existence

(a) Spurious Speculations

Pre-existence is the speculation that souls existed in a former world. The student cannot be too careful about these speculations. There is no book which lends itself more readily to speculation than the Bible, and yet all through, the Bible warns against it. By *speculation* we mean taking a series of facts and weaving all kinds of fancies round them. In Deuteronomy 29:29: "The secret things belong to the LORD our God, but those things which are revealed belong to us and to our children for ever," and Revelation 5:3: "And no one in heaven or on the earth or under the earth was able to open the scroll, or to look at it," the bounds of human knowledge with regard to biblical revelation

---

2. N.B.: Spiritualism is the great soul crime. Sickness, natural and demoniacal, will be examined.

are fairly well marked. What is revealed in God's Book is for us; what is not revealed is not for us. *Speculation* is searching into what is not revealed.

The subject of pre-existence as it is popularly taught is not revealed in God's Book; it is a speculation based on certain things said in God's Book. Theosophy lends itself largely to speculation, and all theosophical and occult speculations are ultimately dangerous to the mental, moral, and spiritual balance. Speculate if you care to, but never teach any speculation as a revelation from the Bible.

Speculation comes right down to our lives in very enticing ways. Telepathy is one enticing way in which the speculation of transmigration and pre-existence is introduced to our minds. *Telepathy* means being able to discern someone else's thought by my own. This opens up the line of autosuggestion. If one individual can suggest thoughts to another individual, then Satan can do the same, and the consciousness of autosuggestion on the human side opens the mind to it diabolically. Telepathy is mentioned because all these occult things come down to our lives in seemingly harmless phases.

For instance, spiritualism comes by way of palmistry, reading fortunes in teacups or in cards by planchette, and so on, and people say there is no harm in any of these things. There is all the harm and the backing up of the devil in them. Nothing awakens curiosity more quickly than reading fortunes in teacups or by cards. The same is true of all theosophical speculations, they come right down to our lives on the line of things which are wrongly called *psychology* and awaken an insatiable curiosity. It has already been stated that the Bible does not teach pre-existence.

(b) Startling Scriptures

And yet we have some startling Scriptures which appear to contradict that statement: Jeremiah 1:5; Romans 9:11–13;

and Luke 1:41. We have called these *startling* Scriptures for the obvious reason that they look as if the Bible does teach pre-existence.

There is, however, what may be termed a false and a true idea of pre-existence. The false idea of pre-existence is that we existed as human beings before we came into this world; the true idea is pre-existence in the mind of God. It is not an easy subject to state, but it is one which is revealed in Scripture, that is, the pre-existence in the mind of God not only with regard to the great fact of the human race, but with regard to individual lives. Individual lives are the expression of a preexisting idea in the mind of God; this is the true idea of pre-existence. Call it ideal, or call it what you like, but it is revealed in God's Book. In the few passages listed above, and in a great many more, the idea of pre-existence in the Divine mind is clearly revealed.

There is one other thing in regard to individual spiritual experience: that our individual lives can be, and ought to be, manifest answers to the ideas in God's mind. "A man's steps are of the LORD; how then can a man understand his own way?" (Proverbs 20:24). This gives a lofty dignity as well as a great carefulness to human lives. The expression of it in the life of our Lord is becoming familiar to us, that He never worked from His right to Himself; He never performed a miracle because He wanted to express how able He was; He never spoke in order to show how wonderful was His insight into God's truth. He said, "The Son can do nothing of Himself" (John 5:19). He always worked from His Father (John 14:10).

There are racial memories which obtrude themselves into the consciousness whereby a person may be distinctly conscious of a form of life he never lived, it may be a form of life centuries past. The explanation of this does not lie in the fact that that particular individual lived centuries ago, but that his progenitors did, and there are traces in his nerve substance which by one of the incalculable tricks of individual experience may suddenly emerge into consciousness.

(c) Steadying Scriptures

By this we mean those Scriptures which hold our minds to some steady line of interpretation.

(1) No Soul before Body

In the creation of the human being, the Bible reveals that his body was created first, not his soul. The body existed before the soul in creation; so we cannot trace the history or the destiny of the human soul before the creation of the human race. This is the first main general line of revelation. We have in Genesis 1:26 a splendid example of true pre-existence. God deliberately said what was in His mind before He created man—"Let Us make man in Our image, according to Our likeness"—the pre-existence of humanity in the mind of God.

(2) No Soul Destiny Pre-Adamic

"Therefore, just as through one man sin entered the world, and death through sin, and thus death spread to all men, because all sinned" (Romans 5:12). Soul destiny began with the human race, not before it. Take any passage which deals with individual destiny—Ezekiel 18, for instance—and you will find that destiny is determined in the lifetime of the individual soul. All speculations regarding the transmigration of souls are alien to the teaching of the Bible.

(3) No Soul but by Procreation

We are not created directly by the hand of the Almighty as Adam was; we are procreated, generated, and each person's spirit, soul, and body all come together in embryo, as related elsewhere.

(d) The Pre-existence of Our Lord

"And now, O Father, glorify Me together with Yourself, with the glory which I had with You before the world was" (John 17:5).

This pre-existence is quite different from the phase of pre-existence previously mentioned. This is the existence of a Being who was known before He came here, and the reason of His coming here is explained by what He was before He came. This is the only case of the pre-existence of a Person in a former life. The Bible nowhere teaches that individuals existed in a world before they came here; the only pre-existence is in the Divine mind.

2. Present Existence

Now we come down to simple ground where we are at home. In the last chapter we dealt with something of the nature of the complex characteristics of the soul, more perplexing and whirling and confusing the more we think of them. When we begin to think of the possibilities of the human soul, no clear thought is possible at first.

We come now to the possibilities and capacities of the soul. Can these be satisfied here and now? The Bible says they can. The claim of the salvation of Jesus Christ is that the Spirit of God can satisfy the last aching abyss of the human soul, not only hereafter, but here and now. Satisfaction does not mean stagnation; satisfaction is the knowledge that we have gained the right type of life for our souls.

(a) Satisfaction of the Soul

"O bless our God, you peoples. . . . Who keeps our soul among the living, and does not allow our feet to be moved" (Psalm 66:8–9; see also Psalm 66:12, 16; Isaiah 55:3). These are indications from among innumerable passages in God's Book which prove that this complex soul which we have been examining can be satisfied and placed in perfect harmony with itself and with God in its present existence. The thought that a human soul can fulfill the predestined purpose of God is a great one.

The human soul, however, can also be stagnated by ignorance. In the beginning, we do not know the capabilities of our souls and are content to be ignorant; but when we come under conviction of sin, we begin to understand the awful, unfathomable depths of our natures and the claim of Jesus Christ that He can satisfy this abyss. Everyone who knows what his soul is capable of, knows its possibilities and terrors, but knows also the salvation of God, will bear equal testimony with the written Word of God that Jesus Christ can satisfy the living soul. Isaiah 55:3 is our Lord's message to the age in which we live—"Incline your ear, and come to Me. Hear, and your souls shall live; and I will make an everlasting covenant with you—the sure mercies of David."

Bear in mind that the devil does satisfy for a time. "Their eyes bulge with abundance; they have more than heart could wish" (Psalm 73:7). "Because they do not change, therefore they do not fear God" (Psalm 55:19).

(b) Sins and Surroundings of the Soul

Psalm 6 refers to the surroundings of the soul in bodily sickness and perplexity and the inward results of these. The psalmist's first degree of prayer is, "Heal me, for my bones are troubled"; the second degree is, "Heal me . . . . My soul also is greatly troubled," and the third degree is, "Save me for Your mercies' sake" (Psalm 6:24). These are three degrees of perplexity arising from the soul's surroundings: because of pain, because the mental outlook is cloudy, and because God has not said a word.

When the soul is perplexed—and it certainly will be if we are going on with God, because we are a mark for Satan—and the sudden onslaught comes, as it did in the life of Job, we cry, "Heal me because of my pain," but there is no answer. Then we cry, "Heal me, not because I am in pain, but because my soul is perplexed; I cannot see any way out of it or why this thing should be"; still no answer; then at last we cry, "Heal me, O Lord, not because of my pain, nor because my soul is sick, but for Your mercies' sake." Then we have the answer, "The LORD has heard my supplication" (Psalm 6:9).

The surroundings of the soul, the scenes which arise from our doings, do produce perplexity in the soul. The soul cannot be separated from the body, and bodily perplexities produce difficulties in the soul, and these difficulties go inward and at times intrude right to the very throne of God in the heart.

"Behold, all souls are Mine; . . . the soul who sins shall die" (Ezekiel 18:4). In this passage the soul life and the sin that is punished are connected. The inherited disposition of sin must be cleansed, but for every sin we commit we are punished. "Receiving the end of your faith—the salvation of your souls" (1 Peter 1:9). *Salvation* refers to the whole gamut of a person, spirit, soul, and body; "Christ the firstfruits" (1 Corinthians 15:23), with the ultimate reach in the hereafter of our spirits, souls, and bodies being like His in a totally new relationship. The soul in the present life can be satisfied in all its perplexities, and in all onslaughts and dangers it is kept by the power of God. Sin destroys the power of the soul to know its sin, punishment brings awakening, self-examination brings chastisement and saves the soul from sleeping sickness, and brings it into a healthy satisfaction.

In 1 Corinthians 11:30, "For this reason many are weak and sick among you, and many sleep," Paul alludes to sickness which has a moral and not a physical source. The immediate connection is the obscene conduct at the Lord's Supper of former heathen converts, and Paul says that that is the cause of their bodily sickness. The truth laid down abides, that certain types of moral disobedience produce sicknesses that physical remedies cannot touch; obedience is the only cure. For instance, nothing can touch the sicknesses produced by tampering with spiritualism; there is only one cure—yielding to the Lord Jesus Christ.

(c) Supernatural Setting for the Soul

"Lord, do You want us to command fire to come down from heaven and consume them?" (Luke 9:54). The disciples knew Jesus Christ well enough to know that He had intimacy with supernatural powers, but they had yet to learn that it is possible to scathe sin and at the same time serve one's self. "But He turned and rebuked them, and said, 'You do not know what manner of spirit you are of'" (Luke 9:55). It is possible to do right in the wrong spirit. These were the very people who a little while afterwards asked that they might sit, "one on Your right hand, and the other on Your left, in Your glory"; and one of them was sent down by God to Samaria, where he realized what the fire was that God was to send, that is, the first of the Holy Spirit (see Acts 8).

"For we do not wrestle against flesh and blood, but against principalities, against powers" (Ephesians 6:12). This has to do not with the bodily side of things, but with the supernatural. We are surrounded immediately by powers and forces which we cannot discern physically. "I do not want you to have fellowship with demons. You cannot drink the cup of the Lord and the cup of demons" (1 Corinthians 10:20–21). You can always tell whether Christians are spiritually minded by their attitude to the supernatural. The modern attitude to demon possession is very instructive; so many take the attitude that there is no such thing as demon possession, and infer that Jesus Christ Himself knew quite well that there was no such thing, not seeing that by such an attitude they put themselves in the place of the superior person, and claim to know all the private opinions of the Almighty about iniquity.

Jesus unquestionably did believe in the fact of demon possession. The New Testament is full of the supernatural; Jesus Christ continually looked on scenery we do not see, and saw supernatural forces at work. "Test the spirits, whether they are of God" (1 John 4:1). The human soul may be vastly complicated by interference from the supernatural, but Jesus Christ can guard us there.

Sickness, natural and demoniacal. By natural sickness we mean that which comes from natural causes, not through the interference of any supernatural force. Demoniacal sickness comes from certain parts of the body being infested by demons. Read the records of our Lord casting out demons. Sometimes He said "Deaf and dumb spirit, I command you, come out of him" (Mark 9:25); at other times He said nothing about demons when He healed the deaf and dumb (for example, see Matthew 9:32). In addressing the demon-possessed our Lord frequently mentioned the particular organ affected, but in the case of the man of Gadara, he was possessed by demons not only in a particular organ but through the whole of his body. How much room does thought take up? None! How many thoughts can we have in our brains? Why, countless! How much room does personality take up? None! How many personalities can there be in one body? Take this man of Gadara. "Jesus asked him, saying, 'What is your name?' And he said, 'Legion'; because many demons had entered him" (Luke 8:30).

The case of Judas instances the identification of a human soul with the devil himself. Just as someone may become identified with Jesus Christ so he can be identified with the devil. Just as a man can be born again into the kingdom where Jesus Christ lives and moves and has His being and can become identified with Him in entire sanctification, so he can be born again, so to speak, into the devil's kingdom and be entirely consecrated to the devil. "Satan entered him" (John 13:27). "Did I not choose you, the twelve," said Jesus, "and one of you is a devil?" (John 6:70). This subject awakens tremendous terrors, but these are facts revealed in God's Book. There are supernatural sicknesses of the body and soul in this present life, but Jesus Christ can deal with them all.

3. Perpetual Existence
(a) Mortal Aspect of the Soul

"What is your life? Is it even a vapor that appears for a little time and then vanishes away" (James 4:14; see also Job 14:2). By *mortal* is meant in this order of things only. All through God's Book the soul and the human being as he appears now is described as mortal in one aspect. The soul is the holder of the body and spirit together, and when the spirit goes back to God who gave it, the soul disappears. In the resurrection there is another body, a body impossible to describe in words, either a glorified body or a damnation body: "For the hour is coming in which all who are in the graves will hear His voice and come forth—they who have done good, to the resurrection of life, and those who have done evil, to the resurrection of condemnation" (John 5:28–29), and instantly the soul is manifested again. We have not a picture of the "resurrection of condemnation"; yet our Lord states that there will be such a thing (see also Luke 16:19–31).

We have a picture of the "resurrection of life" in the resurrected body of our Lord. "Who will transform our lowly body that it may be conformed to His glorious body" (Philippians 3:21). The soul life, then, is entirely dependent upon the body.

The indelible characteristics of the individual are in his spirit; and our Lord, who is "the firstfruits" (1 Corinthians 15:23), was spirit, soul, and body. Therefore resurrection does not refer to spirit, that is, personality—that never dies, but to body and soul. "It is sown a natural body, it is raised a spiritual body" (1 Corinthians 15:44). God raises an incorruptible glorified body like His own Son's—"every man in his own regiment," and Jesus Christ leading. Just as the glorified body of our Lord could materialize during those forty days, so will our bodies be able to materialize in the day yet to be.

(b) Immortal Aspect of the Soul

The mortal aspect is strong in the Bible, and the immortal aspect is just as strong. The annihilationists build all their teaching on the mortal aspect; they give proof after proof that because the soul and body are mortal only those who are born again of the Spirit are immortal. The Bible reveals that there is everlasting damnation as well as everlasting life. Nothing can be annihilated. In Scripture the word *destroy* never means "annihilate."

In this present bodily aspect the soul is mortal, but in another aspect it is immortal, for God sees the soul in its final connection with spirit in the resurrection. See Luke 16:25–26, "Son, remember," and 23:43, "And Jesus said to him, 'Assuredly, I say to you, today you will be with Me in Paradise.'" Both these passages refer to the state immediately after death, and reveal that the human spirit—personality—never sleeps and never dies in the sense that body and soul do.

The "soul-sleep" heresy creeps in here. The Bible nowhere says the soul sleeps; it says that the body sleeps but never the personality; the moment after death, unhindered consciousness is the state.

(c) Eternal Life and Eternal Death of the Soul

"For the wages of sin is death, but the gift of God is eternal life in Jesus Christ our Lord" (Romans 6:23; see also Matthew 10:28; Romans 5:21). We have no more ground for saying that there is eternal life than we have for saying there is eternal death. If Jesus Christ means by "eternal life," unending conscious knowledge of God, then eternal death must be never-ending conscious separation from God. The destruction of a soul in hades, or hell, is the destruction of the last strand of likeness to God.

Mark uses a strange phrase: "salted with fire" (Mark 9:49 KJV)—that is, preserved in eternal death. In Romans 8:6, Paul tells us what death is—"to be carnally minded is death." The people put themselves in an untenable position who say that eternal damnation is not personal but that eternal life is. We know no more about the one than we do about the other, and we know nothing about either except for what the Bible tells us.

Probably the greatest book on this subject, apart from the Bible, is the one entitled, *Human Personality and Its Survival of Bodily Death,* by Dr. F. W. H. Myers. It was written during the last few years by a great man who tried to prove, not from God's Book, but simply from speculation, that the human soul is immortal, and he ends exactly where he begins, that is, with his intuitions. All we know about eternal life, about hell and damnation, the Bible alone tells us. If we say that God is unjust because He reveals perennial death and if we imply that the Bible therefore does not teach it, we put ourselves under the condemnation of those passages in the books of Deuteronomy and the Revelation to which we have already referred. These things transcend reason, but they do not contradict Incarnate Reason, our Lord Jesus Christ, and He is the final authority. All we have hoped to do in these studies of the human soul is to suggest lines of research for the Bible student.

9

HEART: THE RADICAL REGION OF LIFE[1]

1. **Center of Physical Life**
   (a) Life-Power—Psalm 38:10; Luke 21:34
   (b) Life of the Whole Person—Acts 14:17; James 5:5
2. **Center of Practical Life**
   (a) Emporium—Psalm 5:9; 49:11; 1 Peter 3:4
   (b) Export—Mark 7:21–22; Esther 7:5
   (c) Import—Acts 5:3; 16:14; 2 Corinthians 4:6

1. Center of Physical Life

In the Bible the heart, and not the brain, is revealed to be the center of thinking. For a long time science maintained a steady opposition to the Bible standpoint, but modern psychologists

---

1. N.B.: The relative position of *head* and *heart* in the Bible and modern thought will be explained. "The head is to the external appearance what the heart is to the internal agency of the soul."

are now slowly coming to find it necessary to revise their previous unbiblical findings in order to explain the facts of conscious life. The heart is the first thing to live physically, and the Bible puts in the heart all the active factors we have been apt to place in the brain. The head is the exact outward expression of the heart. In the mystical body of Christ, Christ is the Head, not the heart. "Christ is head of the church" (Ephesians 5:23; see also Colossians 2:19; 1 Corinthians 11:3).

Then how can people who are not rightly related to God, whose inward dispositions have not been changed, be part of that body, if Christ is the Head, the true expression of the body, especially in the center of its life?

In the Old Testament the head has the prominence of blessing given to it because it is the outward expression of the condition of the heart. "Blessings are on the head of the righteous" (Proverbs 10:6; see also Genesis 48:14; 49:26; Leviticus 8:12; Psalm 133:2). Other passages refer to "the countenance," meaning not only the face and front of the head, but the whole carriage which is an external expression of the person. The countenance becomes the true mirror of the heart, when the heart has had time to manifest its true life. "Moses did not know that the skin of his face shone while he talked with Him" (Exodus 34:29). "The look on their countenance witnesses against them, and they declare their sin as Sodom; they do not hide it" (Isaiah 3:9; see also Matthew 17:2; 2 Corinthians 3:13; 1 Samuel 16:7).

The Bible puts the head in the prominent position, not the central position; the head is the manifestation of what the heart is like, the outward expression of the heart, as a tree is the outward expression of the root. This is the relationship between the head and the heart which the Bible reveals. Materialistic scientists say that "the brain secretes thinking as the liver does bile," they make the brain the center of thinking. The Bible makes the heart the center of thinking, and the brain merely the machinery the heart uses to express itself. This point is very vital in our judgment of people. Carlyle, for instance, represents the judgment of people by those who do not accept the Bible standpoint on this matter. He judged people by their brains, and came to the conclusion that the majority of the human race were fools. God never judges men and women by their brains; He judges them by their hearts.

The use of the Bible term *heart* is best understood by simply saying "me." The heart is not merely the seat of the affections, it is the center of everything. The heart is the central altar, and the body is the outer court. What we offer on the altar of the heart will tell ultimately through the extremities of the body. The heart, then, is the center of living, the true center of all vital activities of body and soul and spirit. When the apostle Paul says "with the heart one believes" (Romans 10:10), he means by the word *heart* more than we are apt to mean. The Bible always means more than we are apt to mean. The term *heart* in the Bible means the center of everything. The human soul has the spirit in and above it and the body by and about it; but the vital center of all is the heart. When we speak of the heart, figuratively or actually, we mean the midmost part of a person.

The Bible teaching differs from that of science in that it makes the heart the soul-center and the spirit-center as well. In dealing with the Bible the danger is to come to it with a preconceived idea, to exploit it, and take out of it only what agrees with that idea. If we try, as has been tried by psychologists, to take out of the Bible something that agrees with modern science, we shall have to omit many things the Bible says about the heart. According to the Bible the heart is the center: the center of physical life, the center of memory, the center of damnation and of salvation, the center of God's working and the center of the devil's working, the center of from which everything works which molds the human mechanism.

(a) Life Power

"But take heed to yourselves, lest your hearts be weighed down with carousing, and drunkenness, and cares of this life" (Luke 21:34: see also Psalm 38:10). These passages are typical of many others where the heart is revealed to be the center of all life power, physical and otherwise. Anything that makes the heart beat more quickly works toward a higher or lower manifestation of the life; our Lord produces the kind of life that instantly alters the heart life.

There are people you come in contact with who "freeze" you—you cannot think, things do not "go," everything feels tight and mean; you come into the zones of other people and all those bands disappear—you are surprised at how clearly you can think, everything seems to "go" better. You take a deep breath and say, "Why, I feel quite different; what has happened?" The one personality brought an atmosphere that froze the heart not only physically, but psychically; kept it cold, kept it down, kept it back; the other personality gave the heart a chance to expand and develop and surge throughout the whole body.

Taken in the physical domain, if people knew that the circulation of the blood and quickening of the heart life would remove distempers from the body, there would be a great deal less medicine taken and a great deal more walking done. The heart is the center of all physical life and of all the imaginations of the mind. Anything that keeps the physical blood in good condition and the heart working properly benefits the soul life and spirit life as well. That is why Jesus Christ said, "Take heed to yourselves, lest your hearts be weighed down with carousing."

Whenever Paul mentions certain kinds of sins he calls them idolatry. Covetousness is called idolatry because every drop of blood in the life of a covetous individual is drawn away from God spiritually. And so it is by sensuality and drunkenness and vengeance. Vengeance is probably the most tyrannical passion of the carnal mind. The first wonderful thing done by the new life given to us by the Holy Spirit is to loosen the heart, and as we obey the Spirit the manifestation in the life becomes easier.

Satan, however, is as subtle as God is good, and he tries to counterfeit everything God does, and if he cannot counterfeit it, he will limit it. Do not be ignorant of his devices!

(b) Life of the Whole Person

"Nevertheless He did not leave Himself without witness, in that He did good, gave us rain from heaven and fruitful seasons, filling our hearts with food and gladness" (Acts 14:17; see also James 5:5). These passages refer to the power of the heart life. If our hearts are right with God, we realize what is mentioned in Acts 14:17, that everything nourishes and blesses the life. James 5:5 indicates the other side of this truth: "You have lived on the earth in pleasure and luxury; you have fattened your hearts as in a day of slaughter." We can develop in the heart life whatever we will; there is no limit to the possible growth and development. If we give ourselves over to meanness and to Satan, there is no end to the growth in devilishness; if we give ourselves over openly to God, there is no end to our development and growth in grace. Our Lord has no fear of the consequences when the heart is open toward Him. No wonder the Bible counsels to "Keep your *heart* with all diligence, for out of it spring the issue of life" (Proverbs 4:23); Solomon prayed for "an understanding *heart*" (1 Kings 3:9), and Paul says that the peace of God will "guard your *hearts*" (Philippians 4:7).

2. Center of Practical Life

(a) Emporium

"For there is no faithfulness in their mouth; their inward part is destruction" (Psalm 5:9). The phrase "inward part" is simply another phrase for heart, and in Psalm 49:11 the phrase "inner thought" means heart. "Do not let your adornment be merely outward . . . let it be the hidden person of the heart, with the incorruptible beauty of a gentle and quiet spirit, which is very precious in the sight of God" (1 Peter 3:3–4).

The heart is the exchange and market; our words and expressions are simply the coins we use, but the shop resides in the heart, the emporium where all the goods are, and that is what God sees but no other person can see. That is why Jesus Christ's judgments always confuse us until we learn how to receive, recognize, and rely on the Holy Spirit. The way people judged Jesus in His day is the way we judge Him today. The way the Bible is judged and Jesus Christ is judged is an indication of what the heart is like if we have not received the Holy Spirit.

When we receive the Holy Spirit we are in the condition of the disciples after the resurrection: their eyes were opened and they had the power to discern. Before they received the Holy Spirit they could not perceive correctly, they simply recorded physically; they saw that Jesus Christ was a marvelous Being whom they believed to be the Messiah; but after they had received the Holy Spirit, they discerned what they had seen and heard and handled, because their hearts had been put right; the whole shop inside had been renovated and restocked by the Holy Spirit.

Notice the difference in the characteristics of the individual who makes the head the center and the person who makes the heart the center. Someone who makes the head the center becomes an intellectual being, he does not evaluate things at all as the Bible does. Sin is a mere defect to him, something to be overlooked and grown out of, and the one thing he despises is enthusiasm. Take the apostle Paul, or any of the New Testament saints—the characteristic of their lives is enthusiasm; the heart is first, not second. This is the antipodes of modern intellectual life. Mere intellectuality leads to bloodlessness and passionlessness, to stoicism and unreality. The more merely intellectual a person becomes the more hopelessly useless he is, until he degenerates into a mere criticizing faculty, passing the strangest and wildest verdicts on life, on the Bible, and on our Lord.

(b) Export

"For from within, out of the heart of men, proceed evil thoughts, adulteries, fornications, murders" (Mark 7:21–22). This passage is detestable to an unspiritual person, it is in absolutely bad taste, nine out of every ten people do not believe it because they are grossly ignorant about the heart. In these verses Jesus Christ says, to put it in modern language, "No crime has ever been committed that every human being is not capable of committing." Do I believe that? Do you? If we do not, remember we pass a verdict straight off on the Lord Jesus Christ, we tell Him He does not know what He is talking about. We read that Jesus "knew what was in man" (John 2:24–25), meaning that He knew people's hearts; and the apostle Paul emphasizes the same thing—"Don't glory in humanity; trust only the grace of God in yourself and in other people." No wonder Jesus Christ pleads with us to give over the keeping of our hearts to Him so that He can fill them with a new life! Every characteristic seen in the life of Jesus Christ becomes possible in our lives when once we hand over our hearts to Him to be filled with the Holy Spirit.

(c) Import

"But Peter said, 'Ananias, why has Satan filled your heart to lie to the Holy Spirit?'" (Acts 5:3). A Pentecostal liar. That is a terrible statement, a statement with a shudder all through it. Such a lie has never been mentioned in this particular profundity before, but it is mentioned here because it is actually possible for the heart to try and deceive the Holy Spirit. "You have not lied to men, but to God" (verse 4). Our Lord undertakes to fill the whole region of the heart with light and holiness. "For it is the God who commanded light to shine out of darkness, who has shone in our hearts to give the light of the knowledge of the glory of God in the face of Jesus Christ" (2 Corinthians 4:6). Can He do it? Do I realize that I need it done? Or do I think I can realize myself? That is the great phrase today, and it is growing in popularity—"I must realize myself." (If I want to know what my heart is like, let me listen to my mouth, in an unguarded frame, for five minutes!)

Thank God for everyone who has been saved from this perilous path by yielding himself to the Lord Jesus, and asking Him to give him the Holy Spirit and obeying the light He gives!

10

HEART: THE RADICAL REGION OF LIFE

The Radiator of Personal Life I

1. **Voluntary**
   (a) Determination—Exodus 35:21; Esther 7:5; Ecclesiastes 8:11; Romans 6:17; 2 Corinthians 9:7
   (b) Design—1 Kings 8:17–18; 10:2; Psalm 21:2; Proverbs 6:18; Isaiah 10:7; Acts 11:23; Romans 10:1
2. **Versatility**
   (a) Perception—Deuteronomy 29:4; Proverbs 14:10; Isaiah 32:4; Acts 16:14
   (b) Meditation—Nehemiah 5:7; Luke 2:19; Isaiah 33:18; Psalm 49:3; Psalm 19:14[1]
   (c) Estimation—Proverbs 16:1, 9; 19:21; Psalm 33:10–11
   (d) Inclination—Deuteronomy 32:46; Joshua 24:23; Deuteronomy 11:18; Proverbs 3:3

---

1. This includes deliberation and reflection.

3. Virtues and Vices

(a) All Degrees of Joy—Isaiah 65:14; 66:5; Acts 2:46

(b) All Degrees of Pain—Proverbs 25:20; Psalm 109:22; Acts 21:13; John 16:6

(c) All Degrees of Ill-Will—Deuteronomy 19:6; Proverbs 23:17; Acts 7:54; James 3:14

A radiator is a body that emits rays of light and heat. We have used a purely mechanical term in order to picture what the heart is, that is, the center that emits rays of light and heat in the physical frame, in the soul, and in the spirit. The heart physically is the center of the body; the heart sentimentally is the center of the soul; and the heart spiritually is the center of the spirit. By *voluntary* we mean acting by choice; choice is made in the heart, not in the head. By *versatility* we mean the power to turn easily from one thing to another. By *virtues* we mean moral excellencies; by *vices*, immoral conduct.

1. Voluntary

The Bible reveals that the power of choice springs from the heart, and there are two things to be looked at, *determination* and *design*.

(a) Determination

"But God be thanked that though you were the slaves of sin, yet you obeyed from the heart that form of doctrine to which you were delivered" (Romans 6:17; see also Exodus 35:21). These passages are typical of many which prove that the act of choice is in the heart, not in the brain. Impulse in anyone but a child is dangerous; it is the sign of something unstable and unreliable. *Determination* means to fix the form of our choice, and God demands that we use this power when we pray. The majority of us waste our time in mere impulses in prayer. There are many verses in God's Book which refer to this power in the heart to choose voluntarily. Impulse is not choice; impulse is very similar to instinct in an animal. It is the characteristic of immaturity and ought not to characterize men and women. In spiritual matters take it as a safe guide never to be guided by impulse; always take time and curb your impulse, bring it back and see what form a choice based on that particular impulse would take.

"Bringing every thought into captivity to the obedience of Christ" (2 Corinthians 10:5)—that means the harnessing of impulse. We have the power in our hearts to fix the form of our choice either for good or for bad. No wonder the Bible says, "Keep your hearts with all diligence, for out of it spring the issues of life." We never get credit spiritually for impulsive giving. If suddenly we feel we should give a penny to a poor person, we get no credit from God for giving it, there is no virtue in it whatsoever. As a rule, that sort of giving is a relief to our feelings; it is not an indication of a generous character, but rather an indication of a lack of generosity. God never estimates what we give from impulse. We are given credit for what we determine in our hearts to give, for the giving that is governed by a fixed determination. The Spirit of God revolutionizes our philanthropic instincts. Much of our philanthropy is simply the impulse to save ourselves an uncomfortable feeling. The Spirit of God alters all that. As saints our attitude toward giving is that we give for Jesus Christ's sake, and from no other motive. God holds us responsible for the way we use this power of voluntary choice.

(b) Design

Design means planning in outline. "Whereas it was in your heart to build a temple for My name, you did well that it was in your heart" (1 Kings 8:18) is a typical instance of the fact that God gives us credit, not for our impulses, but for the designs of our hearts. God may never allow the design to be carried out, but He credits us with it. When we have had a good dinner and feel remarkably generous, we say, "If only I had a million dollars, what I would do with it!" We do not get credit for that until what we do with what we have is considered. The proof that the design for the million dollars would be worked out is what we do with the ten dollars we have. David planned in his heart what he would do for God, and although he was not allowed to carry it out, God credited him with having the design in his heart. God deals with the designs of our hearts, either for good or for bad.

Character is the whole trend of someone's life, not isolated acts here and there, and God deals with us on the line of character building. Remember, then, that we have the power to fix the form of our choice. "Delight yourself also in the LORD, and He shall give you the desires of your heart" (Psalm 37:4). Desire embraces both determination and design. Some people behave over this verse before God as people do over a wishbone at a Christmas dinner. They say, "Now I have read this verse, I wonder what shall I wish for?" That is not desire. *Desire* is what we determine in outline in our minds and plan and settle in our hearts; that is the desire which God will fulfill as we delight ourselves in Him.

2. Versatility

Versatility is the power to turn from one thing to another; in the natural world it is called humor. The power to turn from one thing to another is due to a sense of proportion. A self-righting lifeboat gives the idea. Sin destroyed this power in the people of God. Read Psalm 106:6, "We have sinned with our fathers." How did they sin? They forgot what God had done in the past, they had no power to turn from their present trying circumstances to the time when their circumstances were not trying; consequently they sinned against God by unbelief. We have the power to turn from deep anguish to deep joy: "O my God, my soul is cast down within me; therefore will I remember You" (Psalm 42:6).

Some people take on the characteristic of always being merry and think they must always keep up that role. Others take on the role of being great sufferers, and never turn from it. In the life of our Lord we find the basal balance of this power; look also at Paul's argument in Romans 8:28: "And we know that all things work together for good to those who love God." We have to take the "all things" when put "together," not in bits. If your circumstances are trying just now, remember the time when they were not trying, and you will be surprised at the self-righting power in the human heart to turn from one thing to another.

How much misery a human heart can stand, and how much joy! If we lose the power of turning from one to the other, we upset the balance. God's Spirit restores and keeps the balance right.

(a) Perception

"A heart to perceive and eyes to see and ears to hear" (Deuteronomy 29:4; see also Proverbs 14:10). *Perception* means the power to discern what we hear and see and read, the power to discern the history of the nation to which we belong, the power to discern in our personal lives. This power is also in the heart. How many of us have the power to "hear with our ears"? Jesus said, "He who has ears to hear, let him hear" (Matthew 11:15). We must have the power of perception in order to interpret what we hear. Isaiah 53:1 puts it in this way: "Who has believed our report? And to whom has the arm of the Lord been revealed?" (KJV).

We all see the common occurrences of our daily lives, but which of us is able to perceive the arm of the Lord behind them? Who can perceive behind the thunder the voice of God? We read in John 12 that when there came a voice out of heaven, the people that stood by said it had thundered; but Jesus recognized His Father's voice. The One had perception, the others had not. The light which smote Saul of Tarsus on the way to Damascus staggered and amazed the people who journeyed with him, but they heard not the voice; Saul knew it to be the Lord and answered, "Who are You, Lord?" (Acts 9:5). The one had the power of perception, the others had not.

The characteristic of a person without the Spirit of God is that he has no power of perception, he cannot perceive God at work in the ordinary occurrences. The marvelous, uncrushable characteristic of a saint is that he does discern God. You may put a saint in tribulation, amid an onslaught of principalities and powers, in peril, pestilence or under the sword, you may put a saint anywhere you like, and he is more than conqueror every time. Why? Because his heart being filled with the love of God, he has the power to perceive and understand that behind all these things is God making them work together for good.

"Turn away my eyes from looking at worthless things" (Psalm 119:37). This does not mean, "Keep my eyes shut," but, "Give me the power to direct my eyes aright." A sheet of white paper can be soiled, a sunbeam cannot be soiled, and God keeps His saints like light. Oh, the power of full-orbed righteousness! Thank God for the sanity of His salvation! He takes hold of our hearts *and* our heads!

(b) Meditation

Meditation means getting to the middle of a thing, not being like a pebble in a brook letting the water of thought go over us;

that is *reverie*, not meditation. Meditation is an intense spiritual activity. It means bringing every bit of the mind into harness and concentrating its powers; it includes both deliberation and reflection. Deliberation means being able to weigh well what we think, conscious all the time that we are deliberating and meditating. "I consulted with myself" (Nehemiah 5:7 KJV)—that is exactly the meaning of meditation; also—"Mary kept all these things, and pondered them in her heart" (Luke 2:19 KJV).

A great many delightful people mistake meditation for prayer; meditation often accompanies prayer, but it is not prayer, it is simply the power of the natural heart to get to the middle of things. Prayer is asking, whereby God puts processes to work and creates things which are not in existence until we ask. It is not that God withholds, but He has so constituted things on the ground of redemption that they cannot be given until we ask. Prayer is definite talk to God, around which God puts an atmosphere, and we get answers back. Meditation has a reflex action; people without an ounce of the Spirit of God in them can meditate, but that is not prayer. This fundamental distinction is frequently obscured. Mary "pondered" these things in her heart—she meditated on them, got right to the center of the revelations about her Son, but as far as we know, she did not utter a word to anyone.

But read John's gospel, and a wonder will occur to you. St. Augustine has called John's gospel, "the Heart of Jesus Christ." Recall what Jesus said to His mother about John: "Woman, behold your son!" and to John about Mary, "Behold your mother! And from that hour that disciple took her to his own home" (John 19:26). It is surely quite legitimate to think that Mary's meditations found marvelous expression to John under the guidance of the Spirit of God, and found a place in his gospel and epistles.

(c) Estimation

"The preparations of the heart belong to man, but the answer of the tongue is from the LORD" (Proverbs 16:1). To *estimate* means to reckon the value. Estimates are made in the heart, and God alters our estimates. To put it practically—those of you who have received God's Spirit and know His grace experientially, watch how He has altered your estimate of things. It used to matter a lot what your worldly crowd thought about you; how much does it matter now? You used to estimate highly the good opinion of certain people; how do you estimate it now? You used to estimate that immoral conduct was the worst crime on earth, but how do you estimate it now?

We are horrified at immoral conduct in social life, but how many of us are as horrified at pride as Jesus Christ was? Do we begin to understand what Jesus meant when He used such words as, "Brood of vipers!" or, "You are like whitewashed tombs" (Matthew 3:7; 23:27)? To whom was He talking? To the scribes and Pharisees! God alters our estimates, and we shall find that God gives us a deeper horror of carnality than ever we had of immorality; a deeper horror of the pride which lives clean among society but lifts itself against God, than of any other thing. Pride is the central citadel of independence of God.

God will also alter our estimate of honor. Everyone has an honor of some sort; a thief has an honor, a gambler has an honor, everybody has an honor of some kind. Jesus Christ had an honor; they called Him a glutton and a winebibber (Matthew 11:19); they said He was beside Himself; possessed with a demon, and He never opened His mouth. He made Himself of no reputation (Philippians 2:7). But let His Father's honor be touched and all was different. Watch His first public ministry in Jerusalem—with a scourge of small cords in His hands over-turning the moneychangers' tables and driving men and cattle out! Where is the meek and mild and gentle Jesus now? His Father's honor was at stake.

Our estimate of honor measures our growth in grace. What we stand up for proves what our character is like. If we stand up for our reputations it is a sign they need standing up for! God never stands up for His saints, they do not need it. The devil tells lies about people, but no slander on earth can alter a person's character. Let God's honor be slandered, and instantly there is something else to deal with in your "meek" saint. You cannot arouse him on his own account, but begin to slander God and a new sense of honor is awakened, a new estimate has been put in. God enables us to have the right perspective, to come to the place where we understand that the things which are seen are temporal, and to estimate them accordingly and to hold a right scale of judgment.

3. Virtues and Vices

(a) All Degrees of Joy

The Bible talks plentifully about joy, but it nowhere speaks about a "happy" Christian. Happiness depends on what happens; joy does not. Remember, Jesus Christ had joy, and He prays "that they may have My joy fulfilled in themselves" (John 17:13).

I want to give one warning concerning Christian Science. There is no objection to what Christian Science does to people's bodies, but there is a tremendous objection to its effect on people's minds. Its effect on people's minds is to make them intolerably indifferent to physical suffering, and in time it produces the antipodes of the Christian character, that is, a hardness and callousness of heart.

All degrees of joy reside in the heart. How can a Christian be full of happiness (if happiness depends on the things that happen) when he is in a world where the devil is doing his best to twist souls away from God, where people are tortured physically, where some are downtrodden and do not get a chance? It would be the outcome of the most miserable selfishness to be happy under such conditions; but a joyful heart is never an insult, and joy is never touched by external conditions. Beware of preaching the gospel of temperament instead of the gospel of God. Numbers of people today preach the gospel of temperament, the gospel of "cheer up." The word *blessed* is sometimes translated "happy," but it is a much deeper word; it includes all that we mean by joy in its full fruition. Happiness is the characteristic of a child, and God condemns us for taking happiness out of a child's life; but as men and women we should have been done with happiness long ago, we should be facing the stern issues of life, knowing that the grace of God is sufficient for every problem the devil can present.

(b) All Degrees of Pain

"Like vinegar upon soda, is one who sings songs to a heavy heart" (Proverbs 25:20). This is simply what has been stated already—preaching the gospel of temperament, the gospel of "cheer up," when a person cannot cheer up; telling him to look on the bright side of things when there is no bright side. It is as ridiculous as telling a jellyfish to listen to one of Handel's oratorios—it would have to be made over again first. It is just as futile to tell a person convicted of sin to cheer up.; what he needs is the grace of God to alter him and put in him the wellspring of joy.

Pain exists in the heart and nowhere else. We try to measure pain in the aggregate; but we cannot. When hundreds are killed in a great accident, we are horrified, much more horrified than when one person is killed. There is no such thing as pain in the mass, pain is individual; nobody can feel more pain than the acme of nerves will give, and the more physical expression there is in pain, the less pain there is. It is by refusing to estimate things in their right light that we misunderstand the direction of pain.

(c) All Degrees of Ill-Will

The deepest-rooted passion in the human soul is vengeance. Drunkenness, sensuality, and covetousness go deep, but not so deep as vengeance. Some such thought as this explains Judas; it says that he "kissed Him" (Mark 14:45). We read of the remorse of Judas, but there was no repentance in it; the end of his life was reached, there was nothing more to live for. There are records of people committing murder after a long line of vengeance and then dying of a broken heart, not because they are penitent, but because there was nothing more to live for.

Vengeance is the most deeply rooted passion in the human soul, and the impersonation of it is the devil. The devil has an absolute detestation of God, an immortal hatred of God. Satan's sin is at the summit of all sins; our sin is at the base of all sins. If sin has not reached its awful height in us, it may do so unless we let God alter the springs of our hearts.

Thank God He does alter the heart, and when His new life is in our hearts, we can work it out through our heads and express it in our lives.

11

HEART: THE RADICAL REGION OF LIFE

The Radiator of Personal Life II

1. **Voluntary**
   (a) Love—1 Timothy 1:5; Proverbs 23:26; Judges 5:9; Philippians 1:7; 2 Corinthians 7:3
   (b) Hate—Leviticus 19:17; Psalm 105:25
2. **Versatility.**
   (a) Memory—2 Chronicles 7:11; Isaiah 65:17; Jeremiah 3:16; Acts 7:23; 1 Corinthians 2:9; Luke 1:66; 21:14
   (b) Thinking—Genesis 8:21; 17:17; 24:45; Ecclesiastes 1:16; Matthew 24:48; Hebrews 4:12
   (c) Birthplace of Words—Job 8:10; Psalm 15:2; Matthew 12:34; Exodus 28:3
3. **Virtues and Vices.**
   (a) All Degrees of Fear—Deuteronomy 28:28; Psalm 113:4; Proverbs 12:25; Ecclesiastes 2:20; Jeremiah 32:40

(b) All Degrees of Anguish—Leviticus 26:36; Joshua 5:1; Psalm 102:4; Jeremiah 4:19

(c) All Conscious Unity—1 Chronicles 12:38; Jeremiah 32:39; Ezekiel 11:19; Acts 4:32

1. Voluntary

(a) Love

"Now the purpose of the commandment is love from a pure heart, from a good conscience, and faith" (1 Timothy 1:5; see also Judges 5:9; Proverbs 23:26; Philippians 1:7; 2 Corinthians 7:3). Love is the sovereign preference of my person for another person, and we may be astonished to realize that love springs from a voluntary choice. Love for God does not spring naturally out of the human heart; but it is up to us to choose whether we will have the love of God imparted to us by the Holy Spirit. "The love of God has been poured out in our hearts by the Holy Spirit who was given to us" (Romans 5:5; see also Luke 11:13). We are emphasizing just now the need of voluntary choice. It is of no use to pray, "O Lord, for more love! Give me love like Yours; I do want to love You better," if we have not begun at the first place, and that is to choose to receive the Holy Spirit who will pour out the love of God in our hearts.

Beware of the tendency of trying to do what God alone can do, and of blaming God for not doing what we alone can do. We try to save ourselves, but God only can do that; we try to sanctify ourselves, but God only can do that. After God has done these sovereign works of grace in our hearts, we have to work them out in our lives. "Work out your own salvation with fear and trembling; for it is God who works in you both to will and to do for His good pleasure" (Philippians 2:12–13).

The love of God is the great mainspring, and by our voluntary choice we can have that love poured out in our hearts, then unless hindered by disobedience, it will go on to develop into the perfect love described in 1 Corinthians 13.

We have, then, to make the voluntary choice of receiving the Holy Spirit who will pour out in our hearts the love of God, and when we have that wonderful love in our hearts, the sovereign preference for Jesus Christ, our love for others will be relative to this central love. "For we do not preach ourselves, but Christ Jesus the Lord, and ourselves your bondservants *for Jesus' sake*" (2 Corinthians 4:5).

(b) Hate

"You shall not hate your brother in your heart" (Leviticus 19:17; see also Psalm 105:25. The passages quoted are chosen from an innumerable number which mention *hate*). The exact opposite to love is hate. We do not hear much about hatred in connection with Christianity nowadays. *Hatred* is the supreme detestation of one personality for another, and the other person ought to be the devil. The Word of God clearly shows the wrong of hating other people; but Paul says, "we do not wrestle against flesh and blood," that is, against bad people, "but against principalities, against powers . . . against spiritual hosts of wickedness" (Ephesians 6:12), behind people. Bad people are simply the manifestation of the power of Satan.

If the love of God were presented as having no hatred of wrong and of sin and the devil, it would simply mean that God's love is not so strong as our love. The stronger and higher and more emphatic the love, the more intense is its obverse, hate. God loves the world so much that He hates with a perfect hatred the thing that is twisting people away from Him. To put it crudely, the two antagonists are God and the devil.

A good way to use the "Cursing" Psalms is in some such way as this—"Do not I hate them, O LORD, who hate You? . . . I hate them with perfect hatred" (Psalm 139:21–22). Ask yourself what is it that hates God? Nothing and no one hates God half so much as the wrong disposition in you does. The carnal mind is *"enmity against God"*; what we should hate is this principle that lusts against the Spirit of God and is determined to have our bodies and minds and rule them away from God. The Spirit of God awakens in us an unmeasured hatred of that power until we are not only sick of it, but sick to death of it, and we will gladly make the moral choice of going to its funeral. The meaning of Romans 6:6 is just this put into Scriptural language— "Knowing this, that our old man was crucified with Him." The "old man" is the thing the Spirit of God will teach us to hate, and the love of God in our hearts concentrates our souls in horror against the wrong thing. Make no excuse for it. The next time you read those psalms which people think are so terrible, bring this interpretation to bear on them.

One other thing, the Bible says that "God so loved the world that He gave His only begotten Son" (John 3:16), and yet it says that if we are friends of the world we are enemies of God. "Do you not know that friendship with the world is enmity with God?" (James 4:4). The difference is that God loves the world so much that He goes all lengths to remove the wrong from it, and we must have the same kind of love. Any other kind of love for the world simply means that we take it as it is and are perfectly delighted with it. The world is all right and we are very happy in it; sin and evil and the devil are so many Orientalisms. It is that sentiment which is the enemy of God. Do we love the world in this sense sufficiently to spend and be spent so that God can manifest His grace through us until the wrong and the evil are removed?

Thank God, these voluntary choices are in our hearts, and they will work out tremendous purposes in our lives. Have I made the voluntary choice to receive the love of God? Have I come to the end of myself? Am I really a spiritual pauper? Do

I realize, without any cunning, that I have no power at all in myself to be holy? Do I deliberately choose to receive from God the sovereign grace that will work these things in me? If so, then I must work them out with glad activity.

2. Versatility

In a previous study we explained *versatility* as the power to turn easily from one thing to another. When you are in difficult circumstances, remember the time when they were not so trying. God has given us this power to turn ourselves by remembrance; if we lose the power, we punish ourselves and it will lead on to melancholia and the peril of fixed ideas.

(a) Memory

As expressive of this great and surprising power, take memory, which resides not in the brain, but in the heart. "Thus Solomon finished the house of the Lord . . . and Solomon successfully accomplished all that came into his heart to make in the house of the LORD" (2 Chronicles 7:11; see also Isaiah 65:17; Jeremiah 3:16; Acts 7:23; 1 Corinthians 2:9).

The brain is not a spiritual thing, the brain is a physical thing. Memory is a spiritual thing and exists in the heart; the brain recalls more or less clearly what the heart remembers. In our Lord's parable (see Luke 16:25) when Abraham said to the rich man, "Son, remember," He was not referring to a person with a physical brain in this order of things at all. There are other passages which refer to the marvelous power of God to blot certain things out of His memory. Forgetting with us is a defect; forgetting with God is an attribute. "I have blotted out, like a thick cloud, your transgressions, and, like a cloud, your sins" (Isaiah 44:22). "All these sayings were discussed throughout all the hill country of Judea. And all those who heard them kept them up in their hearts" (Luke 1:65–66; see also Luke 21:14). In these passages memory is placed in the heart. We never forget save by the sovereign grace of God; the problem is that we do not recall easily. Recalling depends upon the state of our physical brain, and when people say they have a bad memory, they mean they have a bad power of recalling. Paul says, "Forgetting those things which are behind" (Philippians 3:13), but notice the kind of things he forgot. Paul never forgot that he was "formerly a blasphemer, a persecutor, and an insolent man" (1 Timothy 1:13); he is referring to his spiritual attainments: "I forget to what I have attained because I am pressing on to something ahead." As soon as you begin to rest on your oars over your spiritual experience, and say, "Thank God I have attained to this," that moment you begin to go back. Forget to what you have attained, keep your eyes fixed on the Lord Jesus, and press on. People say God helps us to forget our past, but is that true? Every now and again the Spirit of God brings us back to remember who we are, and the pit from where we were dug, so that we understand that all we are is by the sovereign grace of God, not by our own work, otherwise we would be uplifted and proud.

In the case of people with impaired memories, as it is termed, some say it would be better to remove them; to put them to sleep if that were legal. Why do they say this? Because they estimate wrongly; they estimate according to the perfection of the machine. God looks at what we cannot see, that is, at the heart. God does not look at the brain, at what people look at, neither does He sum people up in the way we do. The wonderful thing is that if we will hand our lives over to God by a voluntary choice and receive His Spirit, He will purify us down to deeper depths than we can ever go. Then how foolish people are not to hand over their lives to Him! "He will guard the feet of His saints" (1 Samuel 2:9). He will keep your heart so pure that you would tremble with amazement if you knew how pure the atonement of the Lord Jesus can make the vilest human heart, if we will but keep in the light, as God is in the light. "But if we walk in the light as He is in the light, we have fellowship with one another, and the blood of Jesus Christ His son cleanses us from all sin" (1 John 1:7). We use this verse much too glibly; it is simply God letting the plummet right straight down to the very depths of the experience of a redeemed heart and saying, "That is how I see you"—made pure by the marvelous atonement of Jesus, the last strand of memory purified through the blood of His Son.

(b) Thinking

Thinking takes place in the heart, not in the brain. The real spiritual powers of a person reside in the heart, which is the center of the physical life, of the soul life, and of the spiritual life. The expression of thinking is referred to the brain and the lips because through these organs thinking becomes articulate. "For the word of God . . . is a discerner of the thoughts and intents of the heart" (Hebrews 4:12; see also Genesis 8:21; 17:17; 24:45; Ecclesiastes 1:16; Matthew 24:48).

According to the Bible, thinking exists in the heart, and that is the region with which the Spirit of God deals. We may take it as a general rule that Jesus Christ never answers any questions that spring from a person's head, because the questions which spring from our brains are always borrowed from some book we have read, or from someone we have heard speak; but the questions that spring from our hearts, the real problems that vex us, Jesus Christ answers those. The questions He came to deal with are those that spring from the implicit center. These problems may be difficult to state in words, but they are the problems Jesus Christ will solve.

(c) Birthplace of Words

The heart is the first thing to live in physical birth and in spiritual birth. It is a wonderful thing that God can cleanse and purify the thinking of our hearts. That is why our Lord says, "Out of the abundance of the heart his mouth speaks" (Luke 6:45). The Bible says that words are born in the heart, not in the head. "Will not they teach you and tell you, and utter words from their heart?" (Job 8:10; see also Matthew 12:34).

Jesus Christ said He always spoke as His Father wished Him to. Did His Father write out the words and tell Him to learn them by heart? No, the mainspring of the heart of Jesus Christ was the mainspring of the heart of God the Father, consequently the words Jesus Christ spoke were the exact expression of God's thought. In our Lord the tongue was in its right place; He never spoke from His head, but always from His heart. "If anyone among you thinks he is religious, and does not bridle his tongue . . . this one's religion is useless" (James 1:26), there is nothing in it. The tongue and the brain are under our control, not God's.

Look at the history of words in the different countries of the human race, or take our words today—the words for instance, at the head of these studies, they are all technical, there is no "heart" in them. Compare the language of the Authorized Version of the Bible, which was translated into the language the people spoke. Our modern speech is a great aid to inner hypocrisy, and it becomes a snare because it is easy to talk piously and live iniquitously. Speaking from the heart does not mean refinement of speech merely; sometimes Jesus Christ's speech sounded anything but nice to natural ears, for example in Matthew 23. Some of the words He used, and some applications He made of His truth were terrible and rugged. Read our Lord's description of the heart: "Out of the heart" says Jesus, "proceed"—and then comes the ugly catalogue (Matthew 15:19). Upright men and women of the world simply do not believe this. Jesus Christ did not speak as a human being there. He spoke as the Master of people, with an absolute knowledge of what the human heart is like. That is why He so continually pleads with us to hand the keeping of our hearts over to Him.

There is a difference between innocence and purity. Innocence is the true condition of a child; purity is the characteristic of men and women. Innocence has always to be shielded; purity is something that has been tested and tried and has triumphed, something that has character at the back of it, that can overcome, and has overcome. Jesus Christ by His Spirit can make us men and women fit to face the misery and wrong and discordance of life if we will keep in tune with Him.

3. Virtues and Vices

All degrees of fear, all degrees of anguish, and all conscious unity reside in the heart. Notice how the natural virtues break down, the reason being that our natural virtues are not promises of what we are going to be, but remnants of what we were designed to be. God does not build up our natural virtues and transfigure them. You will often find that when a good, upright worldling is born again, his natural virtues fail, and confusion is the first result of the Spirit of God coming in. Jesus Himself said "I did not come to bring peace but a sword" (Matthew 10:34), that is, something that would divide someone's own personal unity.

There is a difference between the modern way life looking at people and the way the Bible looks at them. The modern way of looking at people and their virtues is to say, "What a wonderful promise of what humanity is going to be; given right conditions, we will develop and be all right." The Bible looks at a person and says, "He must be born again; he is a ruin, and only the Spirit of God can remake him." We cannot patch up our natural virtues and make them come up to Jesus Christ's standard. No natural love, no natural patience, no natural purity, no natural forgiveness, can come anywhere near what Jesus Christ demands. The hymn has it rightly:

> And every virtue we possess,
> And every victory won,
> And every thought of holiness,
> Are His alone.

As we bring every bit of our bodily machine into harmony with the new life God has put within, He will exhibit in us the virtues that were characteristic of the Lord Jesus; the supernatural virtues are made natural. That is the meaning of learning to draw on the life of God for everything.

(a) All Degrees of Fear

"Therefore my spirit is overwhelmed within me; my heart within me is distressed" (Psalm 143:4), "And I will make an everlasting covenant with them . . . I will put My fear in their hearts so that they will not depart from Me" (Jeremiah 32:40; see also Proverbs 12:25; Ecclesiastes 2:20; Deuteronomy 28:28). Fear resides in the heart. Take it physically, if you take a deep breath, you cause your hearts to pump the blood faster through your veins, and physical fear goes; and it is the same with the spirit. God expels the old fear by putting in a new Spirit and a new concern. What is that concern? The fear lest we grieve Him.

(b) All Degrees of Anguish

"I am pained in my very heart! . . . I cannot hold my peace" (Jeremiah 4:19; see also Joshua 5:1; Leviticus 26:36; Psalm 102.4). There again we find that the physical and spiritual center is the heart. All anguish is in the heart. What we suffer from proves where our hearts are. What did Jesus Christ suffer from? The anguish of our Lord's heart was on account of sin against His Father. What causes the anguish of our hearts? Can we fill up "what is lacking in the afflictions of Christ" (Colossians

1:24)? Are we shocked only at social evils and social wrongs, or are we as profoundly shocked at pride against God? Do we feel as keenly as Jesus Christ did the erecting of human self-will against God? The center of true anguish is in the heart, and when God puts our hearts right, He brings us into fellowship with Jesus Christ and we enter into fellowship with His sufferings.

(c) All Conscious Unity

"All these men of war, who could keep ranks, came to Hebron with a loyal heart, to make David king over all Israel; and all the rest of Israel were of one mind [heart KJV] to make David king" (1 Chronicles 12:38; see also Jeremiah 32:39; Ezekiel 11:19; Acts 4:32). The heart is the place where God works, and there all conscious unity resides; when the Spirit of God is in the heart He will bring spirit, soul, and body into perfect unity. Other powers can do this besides God, that is: the world, the flesh, and the devil. The world can give a conscious unity to the human heart; so can the flesh and the devil. The individual who gives way to sensuality, to worldliness, to devilishness, or to covetousness, is perfectly satisfied without God. God calls that idolatry.

We have to watch and see with what our hearts are getting into unity; what our hearts are bringing our souls and bodies into line with. "O LORD our God, masters besides You have had dominion over us" (Isaiah 26:13).

12

HEART: THE RADICAL REGION OF LIFE

The Rendezvous of Perfect Life

1. The Inner
   (a) Highest Love—Psalm 73:26; Mark 12:30–31
   (b) Highest License—Ezekiel 28:2
   (c) Darkened—Romans 1:21; Ephesians 4:18
   (d) Hardened—Isaiah 6:10; Jeremiah 16:12; 2 Corinthians 3:14

2. The Inmost
   (a) The Laboratory of Life—Mark 7:20–23
   (b) Lusts—Mark 4:15–19; Romans 1:24
   (c) The Law of Nature—Romans 2:15
   (d) The Law of Grace—Isaiah 51:7; Jeremiah 31:33
   (e) The Seat of Conscience—Hebrews 10:22; 1 John 3:19–21
   (f) The Seat of Belief and Disbelief—Romans 10:10; Hebrews 3:12

3. The Innermost

(a) The Inspiration of God—2 Corinthians 8:16
(b) The Inspiration of Satan—John 13:2
(c) The Indwelling of Christ—Ephesians 3:17
(d) The Indwelling of Spirit—2 Corinthians 1:22
(e) The Abode of Peace—Colossians 3:15
(f) The Abode of Love—Romans 5:5
(g) The Abode of Light—2 Peter 1:19
(h) The Abode of Communion—Ephesians 5:19

A *rendezvous* is an appointed place of meeting. The heart is the appointed place of meeting not only for all the life of the body physically, but for all the life of the soul and of the spirit. We have seen that the heart is the center of the bodily life physically, the center of the soul life, and the center of the spirit life, and that the Bible places in the heart what modern science puts in the brain.

All through these studies we have insisted on what the Bible insists on, that is, that the body is the most gracious gift God has given us, and that if we hand over the mainspring of our lives to God we can work out in our bodily lives all that He works in. It is through our bodily lives that Satan works and, thank God, it is through our bodily lives that God's Spirit works. God gives us His grace and His Spirit; He puts right all that was wrong, He does not suppress it nor counteract it, but readjusts the whole thing; then begins our work. We have to work out what God has worked in, and we have to beware of the snare of blaming God for not doing what we alone can do. When Paul says, "Be transformed by the renewing of your mind" (Romans 12:2; see also Ephesians 4:23), he is referring to the heart, which is renewed by the Spirit of God. The expression of the heart is made through the mechanism of the brain, and the marvelous emancipation which comes, slowly and surely, is that when God has altered the heart and filled it with a new Spirit, we have the power to will and to do all that He wants us to do.

Jesus Christ puts the test this way: "If you love Me, keep My commandments" (John 14:15), not some of them, but all of them. No one can keep Jesus Christ's commandments unless God has done a radical work in his heart; but if He has, this is the practical, commonsense proof—he keeps the commandments of Jesus.

1. The Inner

The *inner*, the *inmost*, and the *innermost*—we now come right to the very center of our personalities, where we know nothing except what God reveals. God's Book counsels: "Keep your heart with all diligence; for out of it spring the issues of life" (Proverbs 4:23). We are far too complex to understand ourselves; we must hand over the keeping of our hearts to God. If we think that we are simple and easy to understand, we shall never ask God to save us or keep us; but if we have come to the condition of the psalmist, we will hand the keeping of our souls right over to Him and say, "Search me, O God, and know my heart; try me, and know my anxieties" (Psalm 139:23).

(a) Highest Love

We must put the emphasis where the Bible puts it: "God is the strength of my heart" (Psalm 73:26). "You shall love the Lord your God with all your heart, with all your soul, with all your mind, and with all your strength. This is the first commandment. And the second, like it, is this: You shall love your neighbor as yourself" (Mark 12:30–31). According to the Bible, the highest love of the human heart is not for our kind, but for God. Our Lord distinctly taught His disciples that if they were going to live the spiritual life, they must barter the natural for it; that is, they must forgo the natural life. We mean by the *natural* life, the ordinary, sensible, healthy, worldly-minded life. The highest love is not natural to the human heart. Naturally, we do not love God, we mistrust Him; consequently in thinking we are apt to apply to God what should be applied to Satan. Satan uses the problems of this life to slander God's character; he tries to make us think that all the calamities and miseries and wrongs spring from God.

We have defined love, in its highest sense, as being the sovereign preference of my person for another person. The surest sign that God has done a work of grace in my heart is that I love Jesus Christ best, not weakly and faintly, not intellectually, but passionately, personally, and devotedly, overwhelming every other love of my life.

In Romans 5:5, "The love of God has been poured out in our hearts by the Holy Spirit who was given to us," Paul does not say that the capacity to love God has been poured out in our hearts, he says "*the love of God* has been poured out." The Bible knows only one love in this connection, and that is the supreme, dominating love of God. Jesus Christ teaches that if we have had a work of grace done in our hearts, we will show to other people the same love God has shown to us. "A new commandment I give to you, that you love one another; as I have loved you, that you also love one another" (John 13:34).

The natural heart, we cannot repeat it too often, does not want the gospel. We will take God's blessings and His lovingkindnesses and prosperity, but when it comes to close quarters and God's Spirit informs us that we have to give up the rule of ourselves and let Him rule us, then we understand what Paul means when he says the "carnal mind" (which resides in the heart) "is enmity against God" (Romans 8:7). Are we willing for God not to suppress or counteract, but to totally alter the ruling disposition of our hearts? The wonderful work of the grace of God is that through the atonement God can alter the center of my life, and put there a supreme, passionate devotion to God Himself.

The natural individual does not like God's commands; he will not have them, he covers them over and ignores them. Jesus said that the first commandment is: "You shall love the Lord your God with all your heart, with all your soul, with all your mind, and with all your strength." People put the second commandment first: "You shall love your neighbor as yourself." The great cry today is love for humanity. The great cry of Jesus is love God first, and this love, the highest love, the supreme, passionate devotion of the life, springs from the inner center.

What a rest comes when the love of God has been poured out in my heart by the Holy Spirit! I realize that God is love, not loving, but love, something infinitely greater than loving: consequently He has to be very stern. There is no such thing as God overlooking sin. That is where people make a great mistake with regard to love; they say, "God is love and of course He will forgive sin"; God is holy love and He cannot forgive sin. Jesus Christ did not come to forgive sin; He came to save us from our sins. The salvation of Jesus Christ removes the sinner out of my heart and plants in the saint. That is the marvelous work of God's grace.

That the natural heart of the person does not want the gospel of God is proved by the resentment of the heart against the working of the Spirit of God, "No, I don't object to being forgiven, I don't mind being guided and blessed, but it is too much of a radical surrender to ask me to give up my right to myself and allow the Spirit of God to have absolute control of my heart." That is the natural resentment. But oh, the ineffable, unspeakable delight when we are made one with God, one with Jesus Christ, and one with every other believer in this great, overwhelming characteristic of love, when life becomes possible on God's plan!

(b) Highest License

In Ezekiel 28:2, "Say to the prince of Tyre, 'Thus says the Lord GOD: Because your heart is lifted up, and you say, "I am a god," . . . yet you are a man, and not a god,'" we have the presentation of the personality of sin, not the picture of the wrong disposition, which we have all inherited, but of the being who is the instigator behind the wrong disposition inciting to license. *License* simply means, "I will not be bound by any laws but my own." This spirit resents God's law and will not have anything to do with it, "I shall rule my body as I choose, I shall rule my social relationships and my religious life as I like, and I will not allow God or any creed or doctrine to rule me." That is the way license begins to work.

Watch how often the apostle Paul warns us not to use our liberty "as an opportunity for the flesh" (Galatians 5:13), don't use your liberty for license. What is the difference between liberty and license? *Liberty* is the ability to perform the law, perfect freedom to fulfill all the demands of the law. To be free from the law means that I am the living law of God, there is no independence of God in my makeup. *License* is rebellion against all law. If my heart does not become the center of divine love, it may become the center of diabolical license. Do people believe that nowadays? The majority of us do not accept Jesus Christ's statements. When we look at them, their intensity and profundity make us shrink.

A very profitable and solemn study is in the connection of the concept of children of the devil as used by Jesus. "You are of your father the devil, and the desires of your father you want to do" (John 8:44). He is not referring to ordinary sinners, but to religious sinners. Natural sinners are called "children of wrath," but when our Lord referred to children of the devil, He was referring to religious disbelievers, that is, those who had seen the light and refused to walk in it; they would not have it.

Remember the two alternatives: our hearts may be the center of the divine rule making us one with God's thoughts and purposes, or it may be the center of the devil's rule making us one with the prince of this world, the being who hates God, one with the natural life which barters the spiritual.

(c) Darkened

"Although they knew God, they did not glorify Him as God . . . but became futile in their thoughts, and their foolish hearts were darkened" (Romans 1:21; see also Ephesians 4:18). These are striking passages, quite at home in the New Testament, but at home nowhere else. This is not the darkness which comes from intensity of light; it is the refusal to allow any light at all. Read John 3:19 and you will see how our Lord uses the word *darkness*. "This is the condemnation," He says, the critical moment, "that the light has come into the world, and men loved darkness rather than light, because their deeds were evil." On another occasion Jesus said, "If therefore the light that is in you is darkness, how great is that darkness!" (Matthew 6:23). *Darkness* is my own point of view; when I allow the prejudice of my head to shut down the witness of my heart, I make my heart dark.

When Jesus Christ preached His first public sermon in Nazareth, where He had been brought up, the hearts of the people witnessed to Him wonderfully, then their prejudices got in the way and they closed down the witness of their hearts, broke up the service and tried to kill Him. That is an instance of how it is possible to choke the witness of the heart by the prejudice of the head. In John 3 Jesus was talking to a man who was in danger of closing down the witness of his heart because of his Jewish prejudice. Is there any light for which some of us have been thanking God, as the psalmist puts it "God is the LORD, and He has given us light; bind the sacrifice with cords" (Psalm 118:27), and is there a prejudice coming in and closing down the witness of the heart? If so, that is where the darkened heart begins; the light does not shine because it cannot. Until the Holy Spirit comes in we see only along the line of our prejudices. When we let the Holy Spirit come in, He will blow away the lines of our prejudices with His dynamic power, and we can begin to go in God's light.

A darkened heart is a terrible thing, because a darkened heart may make a person peaceful. A person says, "My heart is not bad, I am not convicted of sin; all this talk about being born again and filled with the Holy Spirit is so much absurdity." The natural heart needs the gospel of Jesus, but it does not want it, it will fight against it, and it takes the convicting Spirit of God to make men and women know they need to experience a radical work of grace in their hearts.

(d) Hardened

"But their minds were blinded. For until this day the same veil remains unlifted . . . because the veil is taken away in Christ" (2 Corinthians 3:14). The characteristic of the hardened—blinded—heart is familiar in the Bible but not anywhere else. For instance, we read in Exodus that God hardened Pharaoh's heart. This must not be interpreted to mean that God hardened a man's heart and then condemned him for being hard. It means rather that God's laws, being God's laws, do not alter, and that if anyone refuses to obey God's law he will be hardened away from God, and that by God's own decree. Nobody's destiny is made for him, he makes his own; but the imperative necessity that a person must make his own destiny is of God.

Whenever someone comes into an exalted position, it is a

position in which he can either show the marvelous grace of God, or the hardening of his heart away from God. This is true of the prejudiced heart and the hardened heart, but not so true of the darkened heart. In a hardened heart there is no witness being crushed down; the heart is simply hard and untouched, and when God's love and God's works are abroad, it remains like ice; it may be smashed and broken by judgments, but it is simply breaking ice. The only way to alter the hardened heart is to melt it, and the only power that can melt it is the fire of the Holy Spirit.

The heart is so truly central that God alone knows it, and the illustrations the Bible uses are varied figures in order that we may understand how God deals with the heart.

2. The Inmost

(a) The Laboratory of Life

A laboratory is the place where things are prepared for use. The heart never dies, it is as immortal as God's Spirit because it is the center of the human spirit. Memory never dies, mind never dies; the bodily machine dies, and the manifestation of the heart and life in the body dies, but the heart never dies. "Son, remember," these words were spoken to a man out of the body.

The things prepared for use are prepared in the heart. "From within, out of the heart of men, proceed evil thoughts" (Mark 7:21). These are staggering words, and they spring from the lips of the Master of the human heart. They are not the shrewd guesses of a scientist, or the simple intimations of an apostle; they are the revelation of God Almighty through Jesus Christ. Look at them and see whether they do not awaken resentment in you unless you have received the Spirit of God. This verse means that no crime has ever been committed by anyone that everyone is not capable of committing. How many people believe that?

"It is absurd, morbid nonsense," they say, which means that Jesus Christ did not know what He was talking about. Today people are willingly and eagerly and all-embracingly accepting Christian Science, that popularization of the belief that there is no such thing as sin or suffering or death, that they are all imagination. The consequence is people are preaching the gospel of temperament—"Cheer up and look on the bright side of things." How can a person look on the bright side of things when the Spirit of God has shown him or her the possibilities of hell within? The majority of us are shockingly ignorant about ourselves simply because we will not allow the Spirit of God to reveal the enormous dangers that lie hidden in the centers of our spirits. Jesus Christ taught that dangers never come from outside, but from within. If we will accept Jesus Christ's verdict and receive the Spirit of God, we need never know in conscious life that what He says about the human heart is true, because He will re-relate the heart from within.

Perfect life does not mean perfection. *Perfection* means perfect attainment in everything. Perfect lives mean the perfect adjustment of all our relationships to God, nothing out of joint, everything rightly related; then we can begin to have perfect lives, that is, we can begin to attain. A child is a perfect human being, so is an adult; what is the difference? The one is not yet grown and matured, the other is. Paul puts the two perfections very clearly in Philippians 3:12–15. When you are sanctified you have become perfectly adjusted to God, but remember, Paul implies, that you have attained to nothing yet; the whole life is right, undeserving of censure, now then begin to attain in your bodily life and prove that you are perfectly adjusted to Him.

(b) Lusts

"Therefore God also gave them up to uncleanness, in the lusts of their hearts" (Romans 1:24). What is lust? "I must have it at once!" That is lust. Jesus said that lust would destroy the work of grace He has begun in us; "the desires [lusts KJV] for other things entering in choke the word" (Mark 4:19). The word *lust* is also used in other connections, that is, of the Spirit of God, "the Spirit (lusts) against the flesh" (Galatians 5:17). The Spirit of God who comes in at new birth lusts after this body, must have it at once, for God, and He will not tolerate the carnal mind for one second; consequently when a person is born again of the Spirit, there is a disclosure of enmity against God. No one knows he has that enmity inside until he receives the Holy Spirit. When he receives the Spirit the carnal mind is aroused, and the carnal mind clamors and will not yield to the Spirit. This war is described in Galatians 5:17, the flesh lusting against the Spirit, and the Spirit against the flesh, both demanding "I must have this body at once." To which power are we going to give our bodies? Thank God for everyone who says, "Lord, I want to be identified with the death of Jesus until I know that my 'old man' was crucified with Him."

But watch lust on the other side, watch where it begins. "You ran well. Who hindered you?" (Galatians 5:7). Think what simple things Jesus Christ says will choke His word—"the cares of this world, . . . the desires for other things" (Mark 4:19). Once become worried and the choking of the grace of God begins. If we have really had wrought into our hearts and heads the amazing revelation which Jesus Christ gives that God is love and that we can never remember anything He will forget, then worry is impossible. Notice how frequently Jesus Christ warns against worry. The cares of this world will produce worry, and the desires for other things entering in will choke the word God has put in. Is the thing which claims my attention just now the one thing for which God saved and sanctified me? If it is, life is all the time becoming simpler, and the crowding, clamoring lusts have no hold.

The law of nature, the law of grace, the seat of conscience, and the seat of belief and unbelief are all in the heart.

(c) The Law of Nature

"When Gentiles . . . by nature do the things in the law, these . . . show the work of the law written in their hearts, their conscience also bearing witness, and between themselves their thoughts accusing or else excusing them" (Romans 2:14–15).

(d) The Law of Grace

"Listen to Me, you who know righteousness, you people in whose heart is My law" (Isaiah 51:7).

"I will put My law in their minds, and write it on their hearts; and I will be their God, and they shall be My people" (Jeremiah 31:33).

(e) The Seat of Conscience

Conscience is the "eye of the soul," and the orbit of conscience, that marvelous recorder, is the heart. "Having our hearts sprinkled from an evil conscience" (Hebrews 10:22). God puts the law of grace where the law of nature works, that is, in the heart. Thank God for His sovereign grace which can alter the mainspring of life!

(f) The Seat of Belief and Unbelief

"Beware, brethren, lest there be in any of you an evil heart of unbelief in departing from the living God" (Hebrews 3:12). There the distinction is made perfectly clear—the heart must never be agnostic, the head, if you like, may be. Every Christian is an avowed agnostic. Have you ever thought of that? How do I know God? All I know of God I have accepted as a revelation,

I did not find it out by my head. "Can you search out the deep things of God?" (Job 11:7). Next time you meet some agnostic friend, say something like that to him and see if it does not alter the problem for him. We have to keep our minds open about a great many things. The reason people disbelieve God is not because they do not understand with their heads—we understand very few things with our heads—but because they have turned their hearts in another direction. Why was Jesus Christ so stern against unbelief? Because unbelief never springs from the head but from the wrong direction of the heart.

Can I have the evil heart of unbelief taken out and a heart of belief put in? Thank God, the answer is yes! "I will give you a new heart and put a new spirit within you" (Ezekiel 36:26). Can I have an impure, defiled heart made pure, so pure that it is pure in God's sight? The answer is yes! "The blood of Jesus Christ His Son cleanses us from all sin" (1 John 1:7). Can I be filled with the Holy Spirit until every nook and cranny is exactly under the control of God? Again the answer is yes! "He who is coming after me is mightier than I. . . . He will baptize you with the Holy Spirit and fire. His winnowing fan is in His hand, and He will thoroughly clean out His threshing floor" (Matthew 3:11–12).

Jesus Christ's salvation works first at the center, not at the circumference. No one is capable of thinking about being born, or of how they will live when they are born until they are born; we have to be into this world first before we can think about it. "Do not marvel that I said to you, 'You must be born again,'" (John 3:7). "You must be born into a new world first, and if you want to know My doctrine, do My will," said Jesus. A right relation to God first is essential. How are we to have a right heart relationship to God? By accepting His Spirit, and His Spirit will bring us where we can understand how God's grace works. If any one will receive the Spirit of God, he will find He will lead him into all truth.

3. The Innermost

(a) The Inspiration of God

The inspiration of God may dwell in the innermost recesses of my heart. "But thanks be to God, who puts the same earnest care for you into the heart of Titus" (2 Corinthians 8:16). You may be surprised at the seeming slightness of this passage. The inspiration for benevolence and philanthropy springs from God, and God's Book has some stern revelations to make about philanthropy and benevolence; it reveals that they may spring from a totally wrong motive. The inspiration of God does not patch up natural virtues; He remakes the whole of our beings until we find that "every virtue we possess is His alone." God does not come in and patch up our good works, He puts in the Spirit that was characteristic of Jesus; it is His patience, His love, and His tenderness and gentleness that are exhibited through us. "Whoever eats My flesh and drinks My blood" (John 6:54). When God alters someone's heart and plants His Spirit within, that individual's actions have the inspiration of God behind them; if they have not, they may have the inspiration of Satan.

(b) The Inspiration of Satan

"And supper being ended, the devil having already put it into the heart of Judas Iscariot . . . to betray Him" (John 13:2).

(c) The Indwelling of Christ

The indwelling of Christ—an unspeakable wonder! "That Christ may dwell in your hearts through faith" (Ephesians 3:17). This figure of the indwelling of Christ is very remarkable; we are made part of the mystical body of Christ that Christ may indwell us. The New Testament gives three pictures of Jesus: first, the historic Jesus; second, God Incarnate; and third, the mystical body of Christ, which is being made up now of sanctified believers. By the sovereign work of God and the indwelling Christ, we can show through our lives, through our bodily relationships, the very same characteristics that were seen in the Lord Jesus, so that people may know that we have been with Jesus, and, as our Lord said, "that they may see your good works and glorify your Father in heaven" (Matthew 5:16).

The thought is unspeakably full of glory, that God the Holy Spirit can come into my heart and fill it so full that the life of God will manifest itself all through this body which used to manifest exactly the opposite. If I am willing and determined to keep in the light and obey the Spirit, then the characteristics of the indwelling Christ will manifest themselves.

(d) The Indwelling of Spirit

This is something more explainable. The spirit, soul, and body of the Man Christ Jesus were kept in perfect oneness with God the Father by the Holy Spirit. Study Jesus Christ's life: His uplook to God, that is, His prayer life, was always right; His outlook on people was always right, and His down-look on sin and the devil and hell was always right. He did not ignore any of these facts, as a great many people are doing today, and His Spirit energizing our spirits will produce in us the same characteristics and lift us by His marvelous atonement into the same at-one-ment with God. "That they may be one, just as We are one" (John 17:22), not by absorption, but by identification. This is not the teaching which is prevalent now-adays that we are to be absorbed into one great, infinite Being; each of us is to be made one in identity with Jesus Christ to have a disposition like His; consequently we are interested only in the things in which He is interested, we cannot be appealed to on any other line.

(e) The Abode of Peace

"Let the peace of God rule in your hearts" (Colossians 3:15). This is the peace of God, not peace *with* God. Thank God, there is a peace with God, but this is a different peace.

"Peace I leave with you," said Jesus, *"My* peace" (John 14:27)—that is, the peace that characterized Jesus Christ is to characterize His saints.

(f) The Abode of Love

"The love of God has been poured out in our hearts" (Romans 5:5), not the capacity to love God, but the very love of God. That is what Paul means by those words with which we are so familiar—"I am crucified with Christ: nevertheless I live; yet not I, but Christ lives in me; and the life which I now live in the flesh I live by the faith of the Son of God" (Galatians 2:20 KJV). The faith that was in Jesus is in me; I am identified with Jesus to such an extent that you cannot detect a different spring of life, because there is not one! It is no longer the old disposition that rules me, says Paul, but the disposition that is in Jesus Christ. If you have not the Spirit of God, you will think the apostle is straining language beyond its limit in his effort to express what the Spirit of God does, that is, He alters the ruling disposition, and a person shows himself as entirely changed.

(g) The Abode of Light

"A light that shines in a dark place" (2 Peter 1:19). We have a wonderful picture of light in James 1:17, "the Father of lights, with whom there is no variation, or shadow of turning," nothing to hide. That is the characteristic of God, and the apostle Paul counsels us to "Walk as children of light" (Ephesians 5:8).

(h) The Abode of Communion

The apostle John says, "If we walk in the light as He is in the light, we have fellowship with one another" (1 John 1:7). That is a wonderful description of the communion we shall have. Natural affinity does not count here at all. Watch how God has altered our affinities since we were filled with the Spirit; we have an affinity of fellowship with people for whom we have no natural affinity at all; we have fellowship with all who are in the light, no matter who they are, or to what nation they belong, or anything else—a most extraordinary alteration.

13

OURSELVES:
I, ME, MINE

Ourselves as "Knower"—I the "Ego"

1. **Some Distinctions of Importance**
   (a) Individuality
   (b) Personality
   (c) Egotism and Egoism
2. **Some Determinations of Interest—John 3:2**
   (a) The Ego is Inscrutable—Isaiah 26:9; Psalm 19:12
   (b) The Ego is Introspective—Psalm 139; Proverbs 20:27
   (c) The Ego is Individual—Ezekiel 28:1–4
3. **Some Delusions of Importance—2 Thessalonians 2:7–12**
   (a) The Ego in Delusions of Insanity
   (b) The Ego in Delusions of Alternating Personalities
   (c) The Ego in Delusions of Mediums and Possessions

1. Some Distinctions of Importance

We have divided this subject of ourselves into two: the part that knows, the Ego; and the part that is known, the Me. First of all we will take these distinctions generally—individuality and personality, egotism and egoism, and we shall find that the Bible gives us wonderful insight into these distinctions.

(a) Individuality

Individuality is a smaller term than *personality*. We speak of an individual animal, an individual person, an individual thing. An individual person is one by himself, he takes up so much space, requires so many cubic feet of air, and so forth.

(b) Personality

Personality is infinitely more. Possibly the best illustration we can use is that of a lamp. A lamp unlit will illustrate individuality; a lighted lamp will illustrate personality. The lighted lamp takes up no more room, but the light permeates far and wide; so the influence of personality goes far beyond that of individuality. "You are the light of the world," said our Lord.

Individually we do not take up much room, but our influence is far beyond our calculation. When we use the term *personality*, we use the biggest mental conception we have; that is why we call God a Person, because the word *person* has the biggest import we know. We do not call God an individual, we call God a Person. He may be a great deal more, but at least He must be that. It is necessary to remember this when the personality of God is denied and He is taken to be a tendency. If God is only a tendency, He is much less than we are. Human personality is always too big for us. When we come to examine the next sections and trace the Bible teaching we shall find that we are much too complex to understand ourselves.

Another illustration of personality, more often used, is the following: an island may be easily explored, yet how amazed we are when we realize that it is the top of a mountain, whose greater part is hidden under the waves of the sea and goes sheer down to deeper depths than we can fathom. The little island represents the conscious personality. The part of ourselves of which we are conscious is a very tiny part, there is a greater part underneath about which we know nothing; consequently there are upheavals from beneath that we cannot account for. We cannot grasp ourselves at all. We begin by thinking we can, but we have to come to the biblical standpoint that no one knows himself; the only One who knows him is God. "There is a way that seems right to a man, but its end is the way of death" (Proverbs 16:25).

Individuality, then, is a smaller term than personality. Personality means that peculiar, incalculable being that is meant when you speak of you as distinct from everybody else. People say, "Oh, I cannot understand myself"; of course you can't! "Nobody else understands me"; of course they don't! There is only one Being who understands us, and that is our Creator.

(c) Egotism and Egoism

It is necessary to have a proper distinction in our minds regarding egotism and egoism. *Egotism* is a conceited insistence on my own particular ways and manners and customs. It is an easily discernible characteristic, and fortunately is condemned straightway by right thinking people. We are inclined to over-look egotism in young people and in ignorant people, but even in them it is of the detestable, vicious order. Of *egoism* only good things can be said. It is that system of thinking which makes the human personality the center. The thinking that starts from all kinds of abstractions is contrary to the Bible. The biblical way of thinking brings us right straight down to people as the center. That which puts people right and keeps people right is the revelation we have in God's Book. For instance, the teaching of our Lord and of the apostle Paul continually centers around "I," yet there is no egotism about it; it is egoism. Everything in the Bible is related to the person, to his salvation, to his sanctification, to his keeping, and so forth. Any system of thinking which has the person for its center and as its aim and purpose is rightly called *egoism*.

2. Some Determinations of Interest

The personality of the human is his inmost nature; it is distinct from spirit, soul, and body and yet embraces all; it is the innermost center of someone's spirit, soul, and body. There are three things to be said about the Ego.

(a) The Ego Is Inscrutable

The ego is inscrutable, we cannot understand it or search it out. The Bible says that a person is incapable of searching himself out satisfactorily. "With my soul have I desired You in the night; yes, by my spirit within me I will seek you early" (Isaiah 26:9). There the distinction is made clearly between the inmost personality called "I" and the spirit, soul, and body; and this distinction is maintained all through God's Book. I can search my spirit to a certain point. I can search my soul, but only to a certain point. When someone comes to examine himself he begins to find that he is inscrutable, he cannot examine himself thoroughly. He may make certain arbitrary distinctions and call himself body, soul, and spirit, but he instantly finds that unsatisfactory. Those of you who are familiar with books dealing with this subject will find the word *subliminal* (below the threshold) constantly occurring. Something from below the threshold of consciousness every now and again emerges and upsets our teaching about ourselves.

Our Lord's dealings with the disciples made them conscious

of things in themselves of which they had been hitherto unconscious. For instance, in Matthew 16 we read that Jesus said to
Peter, "Blessed are you," and shortly afterwards He said to him,
"Get behind Me, Satan." Peter had not the slightest notion that
God Almighty had lifted him up as a trumpet and blown a
blast through him, which Jesus Christ recognized as the voice
of His Father; or that a little while afterwards Satan took him
up and blew a blast through him, which Jesus recognized as
the voice of Satan. Again, if Peter had been told that he would
deny his Lord with oaths and curses, he would have been unable
to understand how anyone could think it possible. There are
possibilities below the threshold of our lives which no one but
God knows. Jesus Christ brought His disciples through crises
in order to reveal to them that they were much too big to understand themselves; there were forces within them which would
play havoc with every resolution they made. "Who can understand his errors? Cleanse me from secret faults" (Psalm 19:12).
This verse is simply a type of the revelation running all through
God's Book. We cannot understand ourselves, we do not know
the beginnings of our dreams or of our motives; we do not know
our secret errors, they lie below the region we can get at.

(b) The Ego Is Introspective

Not only are we inscrutable, but we are so built that we are
obliged to examine ourselves. *Introspection* means the direct
observation of the processes of our minds. Along this line people become insane. If you cut a tree in half you can tell by the
number of rings inside how old it is; and one may try to do this
psychically, that is, try to cut one's consciousness in half and
find out how it is made. We are so built that we must introspect.
When a person realizes he is incalculable, he wants to understand himself, and consequently he begins to introspect.

The great chapter in the Bible on wise introspection is Psalm

139; it is a Psalm of Intercessory Introspection. The words are a contradiction in terms, but they exactly convey the meaning of the psalm. The tendency in me which makes me want to examine myself and know the springs of my thoughts and motives takes the form of prayer, "O Lord explore me." The psalmist talks of the great Creator who knows the beginnings of the morning and the endings of the evening, who knows the fathomless deep and the tremendous mountains, but he does not end with vague abstractions; these things are all very well, but they are useless for his purpose: he asks this great Creator to come and search him. "My God, there are beginnings of mornings and endings of evenings in me that I cannot understand; there are great mountain peaks I cannot scale; such knowledge is too wonderful for me, I cannot attain it, explore me, search me out." Or again, he means, "Search out the beginnings of my dreams, get down below where I can go, winnow out my way until You understand the beginnings of my motives and my dreams, and let me know that You know me; and the only way I shall know that You know me is that You will save me from the way of grief, from the way of self-realization, from the way of sorrow and twistedness, and lead me in the way everlasting." The Greek philosophers used to tell us to know ourselves, and Socrates' teaching is exactly along the line of this psalm, but from a different standpoint. Socrates' wisdom consisted in finding out that he knew nothing of himself, and that is why he was called by the Oracle the wisest person on earth. We have to be avowed agnostics about ourselves. We begin by thinking that we know all about ourselves, but a quarter of an hour of the plague of our own hearts upsets all our thinking, and we understand the meaning of the psalmist, "Search me, O God"!

Mark you, God does not search us without our knowing. "The spirit of a man is the lamp of the LORD, searching all the inner depths of his heart" (Proverbs 20:27). God makes a person know that He is searching him. When we come to our Lord, this line explains His attitude toward the human soul, "If I had not come . . . they would have no sin" (John 15:22). If Jesus Christ had not come with His light, and the Holy Spirit had not come with His light people would not know anything about sin. It takes the apostle Paul to use the phrase "sold under sin," and to know the meaning of it. Paul had been searched clean through by the penetration of the Spirit of God.

We are inscrutable, but we are so built that we must introspect. Introspection without God leads to insanity. We do not know the springs of our thinking, we do not know by what we are influenced, we do not know all the scenery psychically that Jesus Christ looked at. Our Lord continually saw things and beings we do not see. He talked about Satan and demons and angels. We don't see Satan or demons or angels, but Jesus Christ unquestionably did, and He sees their influence upon us. The person who criticizes Jesus Christ's statements about demon possession does not realize what he is doing. The people with no tendency to introspect are those described in the New Testament as "dead in trespasses and sins," they are quite happy, quite contented, quite moral, all they want is easily within their grasp, everything is all right with them; but they are dead to the world to which Jesus Christ belongs, and it takes His voice and His Spirit to awaken them.

(c) The Ego Is Individual

By the term *individual*, we mean, first, what we stated at the beginning in distinguishing between individuality and personality; and second, that every person is judged before God as an individual being; what he has done he alone is responsible for.

"The word of the LORD came to me again, saying 'What do you mean when you use this proverb concerning the land of Israel, saying, "The fathers have eaten sour grapes, and the children's teeth are set on edge"? As I live,' saith the Lord GOD, 'you shall no longer use this proverb in Israel. Behold, all souls are Mine; as the soul of the father, so also the soul of the son if Mine: the soul who sins shall die'" (Ezekiel 18:1–4).

This line of revelation runs all through God's Book, and it shows the absurdity of the criticism arising from the fictitious conception that we are punished for Adam's sin. The Bible does not say so. The Bible says that people are punished for their own sins, that is, for sins committed culpably. The Bible says that "through one man sin entered the world," but sin is not an act on my part at all. Sin is a disposition, and I am in no way responsible for having the disposition of sin; but I am responsible for not allowing God to deliver me from the disposition of sin when I see that that is what Jesus Christ came to do. The wrong things I do I shall be punished for and whipped for, no matter how I plead. For every wrong that I do, I shall be inexorably punished and shall have to suffer. The inexorable law of God is laid down that I shall be held responsible for the wrong that I do, I shall smart for it and be punished for it, no matter who I am. The atonement has made provision for what I am not responsible for, that is, the disposition of sin. John 3:19 sums it up: "This is the condemnation" (the crisis, the critical moment), "that the light has come into the world, and men loved darkness rather than light, because their deeds were evil." What is light? Jesus says, "I am the light of the world," and He also said, "If therefore the light that is in you is darkness, how great is that darkness!" Darkness is my own point of view.

In regeneration God works below the threshold of our consciousness; all we are conscious of is a sudden burst up into our conscious life, but as to when God begins to work no one can tell. This emphasizes the importance of intercessory prayer. A mother, a husband, a wife, or a Christian worker praying for another soul has a clear indication that God has answered his or her prayer; outwardly the one prayed for is just the same, there is no difference in his conduct, but the prayer is answered. The work is unconscious as yet, but at any second it may burst forth into conscious life. We cannot calculate where God begins to work any more than we can say when it is going to become conscious; that is why we have to pray in reliance on the Holy Spirit. The path of peace for us is to hand ourselves over to God and ask Him to search us, not what we think we are, or what other people think we are, or what we persuade ourselves we are or would like to be, "Search me out, O God, explore me as I really am in Your sight."

3. Some Delusions of Importance

There are supernatural powers and agencies of which we are unconscious which, unless we are garrisoned by God, can play with us like toys whenever they choose. The New Testament continually impresses this on us. "For we do not wrestle against flesh and blood, but against principalities, against powers, against the rulers of the darkness of this age, against spiritual hosts of wickedness in the heavenly places" (Ephesians 6:12). All that is outside the realm of our consciousness. If we only look for results in the earthlies when we pray, we are ill-taught. A praying saint performs far more havoc among the unseen forces of darkness than we have the slightest notion of. "The effective, fervent prayer of a righteous man avails much" (James 5:16). We have not the remotest conception of what is done by our prayers, nor have we the right to try and examine and understand it; all we know is that Jesus Christ laid all stress on prayer. "And greater works than these he will do, because I go to My Father. And whatever you ask in My name, that I will do" (John 14:12–13).

It is only when these speculations and terrors are awakened in us that we begin to see what the atonement of Jesus Christ means. It means safeguarding in the unseen, safeguarding from dangers we know nothing about. "Kept by the power of God"! The conscious ring of our lives is a mere phase, Jesus Christ did not die and rise again to save that only; the whole human personality is included. We have to beware of estimating Jesus Christ's salvation by our experience of it. Our experience is a mere indication in the conscious life of an almighty salvation that goes far beyond anything we ever can experience.

Second Thessalonians 2:7–12 represents the borderland realm of things which it is difficult to trace. The theme is not an isolated one, it runs all through the Bible and indicates a borderland we cannot step over.

(a) The Ego in Delusions of Insanity

What is insanity? One of the greatest mistakes being made today is the statement that the cases of demon possession in the Bible were cases of insanity. The distinction between the two is made perfectly clear; the symptoms are not even the same. *Insanity* simply means that a man is differently related to affairs from the majority of other people and is sometimes dangerous. Paul was charged with madness (Acts 26:24–25), and the same charge was brought against Jesus Christ—"For they said, 'He is out of His mind'" (Mark 3:21). Have you ever noticed the wisdom of the charge? Both Jesus Christ and Paul were unquestionably mad, according to the standard of the wisdom of this world; they were related to affairs differently from the majority of other people, consequently, for the sake of self-preservation, they must be got rid of. Our Lord was crucified, and Paul was beheaded. When we are imbued with Jesus Christ's Spirit and are related to life as He was, we shall find that we are considered just as mad according to the standard of this world.

Another thing said about insane people is that they have lost their reason; this is technically untrue. An insane person is one who has lost everything but his reason. According to the universal standard, an insane person has lost the relation of the body to his reason, lost the relation of the outside world to his reason, yet he can find a reason for everything. Anyone who knows anything about the diagnosis of insanity knows that this is true.

Read the expositions of the Sermon on the Mount today and you will find some of the cleverest dialectics that have ever been written. The writers try to prove that Jesus is not mad according to the standards of this world; but He is mad, absolutely mad, and there is no apology needed for saying it. Either the modern attitude to things must alter, or it must pronounce Jesus Christ mad. "Seek first the kingdom of God and His righteousness, and all these things shall be added to you" (Matthew 6:33). Volumes have been written to prove that the Lord did not mean that; but He did. Common sense says, "That is nonsense, I must seek my living first, then I will devote myself to the kingdom of God." In 1 Corinthians 1 Paul reasons that in the view of God it is the world that is mad, and that someone only becomes sane in God's sight when he is readjusted to God through the atonement.

(b) The Ego in Delusions of Alternating Personalities

The delusion of alternating personalities (see Mark 5:1–15), is one body being the arena of more than one personality. This is not demon possession entirely, although the case we are taking is such. The incident recorded in Mark 5 is not a case of insanity. You wonder first of all who is speaking; the man with the unclean spirit bows down before Jesus and worships Him, he knows perfectly well that Jesus can deliver him; but as soon as he gets there, the other personality cries out against Jesus Christ, and pleads with Him to deal mercifully with him. There are cases of alternating personalities today, amazing records of someone suddenly disappearing from one part of the country and living a totally different life in another part of the country. The delusions arising from alternating personalities cannot be dealt with by science, but Jesus Christ can deal with them.

(c) The Ego in Delusions of Mediums and Possessions

"Now it happened, as we went to prayer, that a certain slave girl possessed with a spirit of divination met us, who brought her masters much profit by fortune-telling" (Acts 16:16). Paul was grieved because this girl was a medium. A spiritualistic medium commits the greatest psychical crime in the world, that is, the greatest crime against the soul. Drunkenness and debauchery are child's play compared with spiritualism. According to the Bible, it is possible for a man or woman to make himself or herself a medium through which unseen spirits can talk to seen men and women. Beware of using the phrase "Yield, give up your will." Be perfectly certain to whom you are yielding. No one has any right to yield himself to any impression or to any influence or impulse; when you yield, you are susceptible to all kinds of supernatural powers and influences. There is only one Being to whom you must yield, and that is the Lord Jesus Christ; but be sure it is the Lord Jesus Christ to whom you yield. In religious meetings it is the impressionable people who are the dangerous people. When you get that type of nature to deal with, pray as you never prayed, watch as you never watched, and travail in communion as you never travailed in communion, because the soul that is inclined to be a medium between any supernatural forces and himself will nearly always be caught up by the supernatural forces belonging to Satan instead of by God. Insanity is a fact, demon possession is a fact, and mediumship is a fact. The Bible says, "False christs and false prophets will rise and show great signs and wonders to deceive, if possible, even the elect" (Matthew 24:24). So beware to whom you yield. When

a nature is laid hold of by the sovereign power of God and recognizes to whom he is yielding, then that nature is safeguarded
for ever. Beware of impressions and impulses unless they wed
themselves to the standards give by Jesus Christ.

"All authority has been given to Me," said Jesus, and "I give
you the authority . . . over all the power of the enemy" (Matthew
28:18; Luke 10:19).

14

OURSELVES:
I, ME, MINE

Ourselves as "Known"—"Me"

1. The Sensuous "Me"—Ecclesiastes 12:13
   (a) My Body—Romans 12:1
   (b) My Bounty—Hebrews 13:15
   (c) My Blessings—Romans 12:13
2. The Social "Me"—Ecclesiastes 7:29
   (a) My Success—Matthew 5:13–16
   (b) My Sociability—John 5:40–44
   (c) My Satisfaction—Matthew 10:17–22
3. The Spiritual "Me"—Ephesians 2:6
   (a) My Mind—Romans 12:2
   (b) My Morals—Matthew 5:20
   (c) My Mysticism—Colossians 2:20–23

By *sensuous* we mean bodily, material consciousness. My Body represents one aspect of "Me." Under the heading of My Bounty, we shall consider our flesh and blood relations, and under the heading of My Blessings, our home, property, and wealth.

Under The Social "Me" we shall consider all that my "class" means: if you insult my class, you insult me. It is important to impress upon ourselves that God recognizes that this is the way He has made us. Our Lord insists on the social aspect of our lives; He shows very distinctly that we cannot further ourselves alone.

The Spiritual "Me" means my religious convictions—my mind, my morals, and my mysticism.

To go back to our first statement: If my body is hurt, I look upon it as a personal hurt; if my home or my people are insulted, it is a personal insult; if my social class is hurt, I consider it a personal hurt; and if my religious convictions are hurt or upset or scandalized, I consider myself as being hurt and scandalized.

The normal "Me," from the Scriptural standpoint, is not the average person. *Normal* means regular, exact, perpendicular, everything according to rule. *Abnormal* means irregular, away from the perpendicular; and *supernormal* means that which goes beyond regular experience, not contradicting it, but transcending it. Our Lord represents the supernormal. Through the salvation of Jesus Christ we partake of the normal, regular, upright; apart from His salvation we are abnormal.

We mean by the term *Me* the sum total of all that a person calls his. That means there is no real practical distinction between "Me" and "Mine." My personality identifies Mine with myself so completely that it is not necessary to make a distinction between Me and Mine.

1. The Sensuous "Me"

Let us hear the conclusion of the whole matter:

Fear God, and keep His commandments,
For this is man's all.

(Ecclesiastes 12:13)

This verse is the conclusion from the point of view of human and divine wisdom as to what is the whole end of life, that is, "to fear God and keep His commandments."

Sensuous means that which is affected through our senses, or that which we get at through our senses. The first thing we get at through our senses is the body. The Bible has a great deal to tell us about our bodies. The main point to emphasize is that the Bible reveals that our bodies are the medium through which we develop our spiritual lives. In the Middle Ages the body was looked upon as a clog, a hindrance, an annoyance, something that kept the person back and upset his or her higher calling; something which had sin in the very corpuscles of its blood, in the cells of its makeup. The Bible entirely disproves this view; it tells us that the body is "the temple of the Holy Spirit," not a thing to be despised. The Bible gives the body a very high place indeed.

(a) My Body

"I beseech you therefore, brethren, by the mercies of God, that you present your bodies a living sacrifice" (Romans 12:1). The apostle does not say, "Present your all'"; the "Higher Life" hymns do that, consequently they are unsatisfactory for you can never know when you have given your all. Look at it in the light of the last chapter, if personality is too big for us to understand, how are we to know when we have presented our all? The Bible never says any thing so vague as "present your all," but, "present your bodies." There is nothing ambiguous or indefinite about that statement, it is definite and clear. The *body* means only one thing to us all, that is, this flesh and blood body.

Ask yourself this practical question: Who is the ruling person that is manifested through my body, through my hands, through my tongue, through my eyes, through my thinking and loving? Is it a self-realizing person, or a Christ-realizing person? The body is to be the temple of the Holy Spirit, the medium for manifesting the marvelous disposition of Jesus Christ all through. Instead of our bodies being hindrances to our development, it is only through our bodies that we are developed. We express our character through our bodies; you cannot express a character without a body. When we speak of character we think of a flesh and blood thing; when we speak of disposition we think of something that is not flesh and blood. Through the atonement God gives us the right disposition; that disposition is inside our bodies, and we have to manifest it in character through our bodies and by means of our bodies. The meaning of bodily control is that the body is the obedient medium for expressing the right disposition. The Bible, instead of ignoring the fact that we have a body, exalts it. "Or do you not know that your body is the temple of the Holy Spirit who is in you?" (1 Corinthians 6:19). "If anyone defiles the temple of God, God will destroy him" (1 Corinthians 3:17). Instead of the Bible belittling the laws of health and bodily uprightness and cleanliness, it insists on these by implication far more than modern science does by explicit statement. Go back again to our first subject, that is, "The Making of Man," and you will recall that the chief glory of the human being is not that he is in the image of God spiritually, but that he is made "of the earth, earthy." This is not a person's humiliation but his glory, because through his mortal body is to be manifested the wonderful life and disposition of Jesus Christ. "Christ in you, the hope of glory" (Colossians 1:27).

(b) My Bounty

"Therefore by Him let us continually offer the sacrifice of

praise to God, that is, the fruit of our lips, giving thanks to His name" (Hebrews 13:15). This verse comes in a chapter which is intensely practical, and which deals with our relationship to strangers as well as our relationships in the most intimate and practical matters of life. The next relationship of my body is my blood relations, my father and mother, my sister and brother, and my wife. Have you ever noticed that these are the relationships Jesus Christ refers to most often? Over and over again when Our Lord tells us about discipleship, that is the sphere He deals with; He puts the relationships in this sphere as crucial. Read Luke 14:26–27, 33, there our Lord places our love for Him away beyond our love for father and mother; in fact, He uses a tremendous word: "If anybody comes to Me, and does not *hate* his father, and mother, . . . he cannot be My disciple." That word *hate* appears to be a stumbling block to a great number of people. It is quite conceivable that many persons have such a slight regard for their fathers and mothers that it is nothing to them to separate from them; but the word *hate* shows by contrast the kind of love we ought to have for our parents, an intense love; yet, says Jesus, our love for Him is to be so intense that every other relationship is hatred in comparison if it should conflict with His claims.

Love for the Lord is not an ethereal, intellectual, dreamlike thing; it is the most intense, the most vital, the most passionate love of which the human heart is capable. The realization of such a fathomless love is rarely conscious, saving in some supreme crisis akin to martyrdom. In the generality of our days our love for God is too deeply imbedded to be conscious; it is neither joy nor peace, it is "Me" obsessed by God in the unconscious domain. Love, to be love, is deeper than I am conscious of, and is only revealed by crisis. This intense personal love is the only kind of love there is, not Divine *and* human love.

Jesus preached His first sermon in Nazareth, where He had

been brought up, and He told His disciples they were to begin at Jerusalem. Did Jesus Christ have such great success in Nazareth where He was known? No, He had exactly the opposite. When they heard Him speak they were so filled with wrath that they broke up the service and tried to kill Him. Our Lord insists that we begin at "Jerusalem" for the sake of our own characters, and our Jerusalem is unquestionably among the bounties of our own particular flesh and blood relations. It is infinitely easier to offer the sacrifice of praise before strangers than among our own flesh and blood. That is where the *sacrifice* of praise comes in, and that is what young converts want to skip. It is by testifying to our own flesh and blood that we are confirmed in our own characters and in our relationship to Jesus Christ. It is recorded in Luke 4:23–27 that Jesus spoke words which maddened His own people; He said, in effect, "It is God's way to send His message through strangers before that message is accepted." They would not accept it from Him. Why? Because they knew Him, and if we look into that statement we shall find that it revolutionizes a great many of our conceptions. We should naturally have said that if Jesus had testified among His own people, they would have gladly received Him; the only place in which they did not receive Him, the place in which He could not do many mighty works, was the place where He was brought up. The place in which Jesus tells us as His disciples to begin our work is among our own flesh and blood, that is our Jerusalem; there we shall get consolidated and know where the true basis of our lives lies. We do not often put together the words *sacrifice* and *praise*. *Sacrifice* means giving the best we have, and it embraces an element of cost. Our own flesh and blood relationships have to be the scene of the sacrifice of praise on our part, whether it is accepted or not. That is where the sacrifice of praise comes in.

(c) My Blessings

By *blessings* we mean our homes and our property. "Distributing to the needs of the saints; given to hospitality" (Romans 12:13). The Bible has a great deal to say about hospitality and entertaining strangers. God recognizes the enormous importance of our immediate circle. The term *blessings* includes my home and my property, all that I distinctly look upon as mine, and I have to use it with this outlook of hospitality, and when I do, I find how personal it is. If any stranger finds fault with my home or insults it, my resentment is intense. My home is guarded in exactly the same way as my body is guarded. It is mine, therefore it is part of the very makeup of my personality, and God will not allow me to be exclusive over it, I must keep it open, be "given to hospitality."

In the East they know a great deal more about hospitality than we do. By *home* we mean what we specially think of when we mention the word, that is, the most intimate relationships; that is the scene where we are to be given to hospitality. The point is that we are to be "given to hospitality" from God's standpoint; not because other people deserve it, but because God commands it. This principle runs all through our Lord's teaching. My body, my blood relationships, my home—I have to keep all these intimate and right, recognizing the first duty in each one. My body is the temple of the Holy Spirit, not for me to disport myself in or to realize myself. My blood relationships unquestionably have to be recognized, but they are to be held in subjection; my first duty in them is to God; and my home is to be given to hospitality. Have you ever noticed how God's grace comes to those who are given to hospitality, if they are His children? Prosperity in home, in business, and in every way comes from following God's instructions in each detail.

2. The Social "Me"

Truly, this only I have found:
That God made man upright,
But they have sought out many schemes.
(Ecclesiastes 7:29)

The word *schemes* is a quaint one. It means devices arising from human self-love. God made the human being upright, normal, perpendicular, regular; but he has sought out many devices, many ingenious twistings away from the normal. The social "Me" means recognition by my class, and this is a wonderful influence with us all. For instance, a boy who is good and mild to his father and mother at home may swear like a trooper when he is with his peers, not because he is bad or evil, but because he wants to be recognized by that group. This is true all through life, and the Spirit of God recognizes the principle and regenerates it. We must be molded by the class to which we belong whether we like it or not, and God may often alter our special setting. We may affect any amount of individuality, but it remains true that we either grovel or strut, according to our realization of how we are recognized by the class to which we belong. The Book of God is insistent on this; we cannot develop a holy life alone, it would be a selfish life, without God in it and wrong. Jesus Christ was charged with being a glutton and a winebibber because He lived so sociably among people; and in His High-priestly prayer He said, "I do not pray that You should take them out of the world, but that You should keep them from the evil one" (John 17:15). The first place to which Jesus Christ led His disciples after He had said "Follow Me," was to a marriage feast. "We will come to him and make Our home with him" (John 14:23), fellow-ship with the Trinity, that is the Class the Christian is placed in. Therefore our concern is to see that we live according to the recognition of that Class, and do those things which please God.

(a) My Success

Success means to end with advantage. What is the Christian standard of success? Jesus Christ distinctly recognizes that we have to succeed, and He indicates the kind of success we must have. The advantage with which we are to end is that we become preserving salt and shining lights, not losing our savor but preserving health, and not covering our light with a bushel but letting it shine. If salt gets into a wound, it hurts, and if God's children get among those who are raw toward God—every immoral person is an open wound toward God—their presence hurts. The sun, which is a benediction to eyes that are strong, is an agony of distress to eyes that are sore. The illustration holds with regard to the individual who is not right with God; he is like an open wound, and when salt has got into it, the pain stirs him first to annoyance and distress, and then to spite and hatred. That is why Jesus Christ was hated; He was a continual annoyance. Again, nothing is cleaner or grander or sweeter than light. Light cannot be soiled; a sunbeam may shine into the dirtiest puddle, but it is never soiled. A sheet of white paper can be soiled, so can almost any white substance, but you cannot soil light. Men and women who are rightly related to God can go and work in the most degraded slums of the cities, or in the vilest parts of heathendom where all kinds of immorality are practiced without being defiled because God keeps them like the light, unsullied.

(b) My Sociability

Sociability means good fellowship. How insistent God is that we keep together in fellowship! In the natural world it is only by mixing with other people that we get the corners rubbed off. It is the way we are made naturally, and God takes this principle and transfigures it. "Not forsaking the assembling of ourselves together" (Hebrews 10:25) is a Scriptural injunction.

In John 5:40–44 our Lord distinctly indicates that He can have nothing to do with a certain class of people, that is, with the people "who receive honor from one another." He says, in effect, "It is a moral impossibility for that individual to believe in Me." Our Lord is exceedingly good company to the saints— "Where two or three are gathered together in My name, I am there in the midst of them" (Matthew 18:20). Beware of isolation; beware of the idea that you have to develop a holy life alone. It is impossible to develop a holy life alone; you will develop into an oddity and a peculiarity, into something utterly unlike what God wants you to be. The only way to develop spiritually is to go into the society of God's own children, and you will soon find how God alters your class. God does not contradict our social instincts, He alters them. Jesus said, "Blessed are you when men hate you, and when they exclude you, and revile you, and cast out your name as evil, for the Son of Man's sake. Rejoice in that day and leap for joy" (Luke 6:22–23), not for some crotchety notion or faddy idea of your own, or for some principle you have wedded yourself to, but *for the Son of Man's sake*. When we are true to Jesus Christ, our sociability is lifted to a different sphere.

"And raised us up together, and made us sit together in the heavenly places in Christ Jesus" (Ephesians 2:6). We are not raised up alone, but together. All through the social instinct is God-given. From the biblical standpoint, wherever someone gets alone it is always in order to fit him for society. Getting alone with God is such a dangerous business that God rarely allows it unless it means that we come into closer contact with people afterwards. It is contact with one another that keeps us full-orbed and well-balanced, not only naturally but spiritually.

(c) My Satisfaction

These things are applicable in the natural and the spiritual worlds alike. *Satisfaction* means comfortable gratification. There are people who say that if you like a particular thing you must not have it; they think that any satisfaction is a sin. Satisfaction, comfortable gratification, is a good thing, but it must be satisfaction in the highest. Jesus said: "Blessed are those who hunger and thirst for righteousness, for they shall be filled" (Matthew 5:6), that is, satisfied.

Matthew 10:17–22 may seem an extraordinary passage to be taken in this connection. The reason it is taken is that it indicates the only place where satisfaction is found, that is, in doing God's will. These verses are often applied to methods people adopt when they speak at meetings. I remember hearing a man say, "I have not had much time to prepare for this morning's address, so I am going to give you what the Holy Spirit gives me; I hope to be better prepared this evening," and he used this very passage as his justification. When we seek satisfaction from God in the world of people, we shall come in contact with "open wounds," and Jesus says people will hate you, systematically vex and persecute you "for My sake." You will be put in all kinds of difficult places, but don't be alarmed, the Spirit of God will bring to your remembrance in those moments what you should say.

So we end where we began, that the social setting of our lives is The Highest. In secret or in public the one Class we are anxious to please is God the Father, God the Son, and God the Holy Spirit, and the only ones with whom we have real communion are those who have the same dominant note in their lives. "Whoever does the will of My Father in heaven is My brother and sister and mother" (Matthew 12:50).

3. The Spiritual "Me"
And raised us up together, and made us sit together in heavenly places in Christ Jesus. (Ephesians 2:6)

This verse refers to now, not to hereafter.

(a) My Mind

My mind means my particular cast of thought and feeling; if you ridicule that, you hurt me. Whenever a certain type of thought is ridiculed, someone is hurt. "And do not be conformed to this world, but be transformed by the renewing of your mind, that you may prove what is that good and acceptable and perfect will of God" (Romans 12:2). A wonderful thing in our spiritual experience is the way God alters and develops our sensitivity. At one time we were amazingly sensitive to what certain people thought; then God altered that and made us indifferent to what they thought but amazingly sensitive to what other people thought, and finally we are sensitive only to what God thinks. "But with me it is a very small thing that I should be judged of you or by a human court. In fact, I do not even judge myself . . . but He who judges me is the Lord" (1 Corinthians 4:3–4). We have to be renewed in the spirit of our minds for one purpose, that is, that we "may prove what is that good and acceptable and perfect will of God."

(b) My Morals

My morals means my standard of moral conduct. "Unless your righteousness exceeds the righteousness of the scribes and Pharisees, you will by no means enter the kingdom of heaven" (Matthew 5:20). The practical outcome of these words is astonishing; it means that my standard of moral conduct must exceed the standard of the most moral, upright man or woman I know who lives apart from the grace of God. Think of the most upright man or woman, the most worthy person you know who has had no experience whatsoever of receiving the Spirit of God. Jesus Christ says, in effect, that we have to exceed his or her rectitude. Instead of our Lord lowering the standard of moral conduct, He pushes it to a tremendous extreme. We have not only to do right things, but our motives have to be right, the springs of our thinking have to be right, we have to be so unblameable that God Himself can see nothing to censure in us. That is the standard of moral conduct when we are born again of the Spirit of God and are obeying Him. What is my standard of moral conduct? Is it God's standard, or the modern one? The modern standard is summed up in one phrase, self-realization. The two are diametrically opposed to one another, there is no point of reconciliation between them.

(c) My Mysticism

My mysticism means my direct and immediate communion with God (See Colossians 2:20–23). Everyone, whether he is religious or not, has something of this sort whereby he goes directly to God. Mysticism is a natural ingredient in everybody's makeup, whether they call themselves atheist, or agnostic, or Christian. God does not alter the need of human nature, He fulfills the need on a totally different line. We are so mysterious in personality, there are so many forces at work in and about us which we cannot calculate or cope with, that if we refuse to take the guidance of Jesus Christ, we may, and probably shall be, deluded by supernatural forces far greater than ourselves. Jesus Christ's way exalts everything about us, it exalts our bodies, exalts our flesh and blood relationships, exalts our homes, exalts our social standing, exalts all the inner part of our lives, our minds and morals and mysticism, until we have at-one-ment with God in them all.

15

OURSELVES: I, ME, MINE

Ourselves as "Ourselves"—"Self"

The passages alluded to in this outline are exclusively from the New Testament; the student can supply Old Testament illustrations for his own use.

1. **Self—Luke 18:9–14**
   (a) Greatness—Mark 12:31; compare with 2 Thessalonians 2:3
   (b) Groveling—Luke 15:19; Luke 5:8
2. **Self-Seeking—Romans 15:1–3**
   (a) Honor—John 5:41–44; John 8:49
   (b) Humility—Matthew 28:4; Philippians 2:1–4

3. Self-Estimation—John 13:13–17
  (a) Superiority—Philippians 2:5–11
  (b) Inferiority—Matthew 5:19[1]

My self is my conscious personality. "My total self includes the whole succession of my personal experiences, and it therefore includes that special phase of my conscious life in which I think of myself." There are three divisions to guide our treatment of this subject: self; self-seeking; self-estimation.

1. Self

In the final analysis, both greatness and groveling are wrong; one grovels and the other swells in greatness, both are expressive of abnormal conditions. Our Lord never teaches the annihilation of self; He reveals how self can be rightly centered, the true center being perfect love toward God. (See 1 Corinthians 13:4–8). Until self is rightly related there, we either grovel or swell in greatness; both attitudes are untrue and need to be put right. The true center for self is Jesus Christ.

(a) Greatness

"The first of all the commandments is . . . you shall love the LORD your God with all your heart, and with all your soul, with all your mind, and with all your strength" (Mark 12:29–30). This commandment is at the heart of all the revelations made by Jesus Christ. He reveals the right center for self to be God, personal, passionate devotion to Him; then I am able

---

1. N.B.: Important Definitions when considering this material:
  (1) Self—The sum total of all a person can call "Me" and "Mine";
  (2) Selfishness—All that gives me pleasure without considering Christ's interests; (3) Sin—Independence of God.

to show to my fellow human beings the same love that God has shown to me. Until I get there, I take the position for the Pharisee or of the tax collector; I either thank God that I am not an out-and-out sinner and point out certain people who are worse than I am, or else I grovel to the other extreme. Both attitudes are wrong because they are not truly centered. How could the Pharisee in our Lord's parable possibly love his neighbor as himself? It was impossible; he had not found the true center for himself. His center was self-realization, and instead of loving the tax collector he increased his own conceit in every detail of comparison. When I become rightly related to God and have perfect love toward Him, I can have the same relationship to my fellow human beings that God has to me, and can love my fellow human beings as I love myself. When a person gets rightly related to God by the atonement of Jesus Christ, he or she understands what the apostle Paul meant when he said, "We do not preach ourselves," that is, self-realization, "but Christ Jesus the Lord, and ourselves your bondservants for Jesus' sake" (2 Corinthians 4:5).

This is the one thing that keeps a person from taking account of evil. If my love is first of all for God, I shall take no account of the base ingratitude of others, because the mainspring of my service to my fellow human beings is love to God. The point is very practical and clear. If I love someone and he treats me unkindly and ungenerously, the very fact that I love him makes me feel it all the more, and yet Paul says love "thinks no evil" (1 Corinthians 13:5), because self is absorbed and taken up with love for Jesus Christ. If you are going to live for the service of your fellow human beings, you will certainly be pierced through with many sorrows, for you will meet with more base ingratitude from your fellow human beings than you would from a dog. You will meet with unkindness and two-facedness, and if your motive is love for your fellow human beings, you will be exhausted in the battle of life. But if the mainspring of your service is love for God, no ingratitude, no sin, no demon, no angel can hinder you from serving your fellow human beings, no matter how they treat you. You can love your neighbor as yourself, not from pity, but from the true centering of yourself in God.

(b) Groveling

"I am no longer worthy to be called your son. Make me like one of your hired servants" (Luke 15:19). "When Simon Peter saw it, he fell down at Jesus' knees, saying, 'Depart from me—for I am a sinful man, O Lord'" (Luke 5:8). Everyone goes through this stage when convicted of sin; we always have a wrong estimate of ourselves when we are under conviction of sin. The prodigal's estimate of himself went beyond his father's estimate of him, and when we are convicted of sin by the Holy Spirit the same thing happens. The balance is upset, the health of the body is upset, the balance is pushed right out by conviction of sin. Sin puts the self altogether out of center, and the person becomes eccentric.

When the Spirit of God convicts a person, he is wrongly related to everything; he is wrongly related to God, to his own body, to everything round about him, and he is in a state of abject misery. The picture of a person not convicted of sin is exactly the opposite. If you watch the tendencies all around us today you will notice this tendency—ignore sin, deny its existence; if you make mistakes, forget them; live the healthy-minded, open-hearted, sunshiny life; don't allow yourself to be convicted of sin, realize yourself, and as you do, you will attain perfection. There is no conviction of sin, no repentance, no forgiveness of sin in that outlook. The Holy Spirit opens not only my eyes, but my heart and my conscience to the horror of the thing that is wrong within, and when He does, I get to the groveling stage. The psalmist says that conviction of sin makes human beauty "to melt away like a moth" (Psalm 39:11). *Beauty* means the perfectly ordered completeness of a person's whole nature. The Pharisee does not grovel, there is a certain beauty of order about a conceited individual, a conformity with himself; he is of the nature of a crystal, clear and compact and hard. When the Spirit of God convicts him, all that beauty crumbles and he goes to pieces, as it were. Jesus Christ takes the person who has been broken on the wheel by conviction of sin and rendered plastic by the Holy Spirit, and remolds him and makes him a vessel fit for God's glory.

Self, then, is not to be annihilated, but to be rightly centered in God. *Self*-realization has to be turned into *Christ*-realization. Our Lord never taught "Deeper death to self"; He taught death right out to my right to myself, to self-realization. He taught that the principal purpose of our creation is "to glorify God and to enjoy Him forever"; that the sum total of my self is to be consciously centered in God.

2. Self-Seeking

"The reproaches of those who reproached You fell on *Me*" (Romans 15:3). What reproaches fell on Jesus? Everything that was hurled in slander against God hurt our Lord. The slanders that were hurled against Him made no impression on Him; His suffering was on account of His Father. On what account do you suffer? Do you suffer because people speak ill of you? Read Hebrews 12:3: "For consider Him who endured such hostility from sinners against Himself, lest you become weary and discouraged in your souls." Perfect love takes no account of the evil done to it. It was the reproaches that hit and scandalized the true center of His life that Jesus Christ noticed in pain. What was that true center? Absolute devotion to God the Father and to His will; and as surely as you get Christ-centered you will understand what the apostle Paul meant when he talks about filling up "in my flesh what is lacking in the afflictions of Christ" (Colossians 1:24). Jesus Christ could not be touched on the line of self-pity. The practical emphasis here is that our service is not to be that of pity, but of personal, passionate love to God, and a longing to see many more brought to the center where God has brought us.

(a) Honor

"Jesus answered, '. . . I honor My Father, and you dishonor Me'" (John 8.49, see also John 5:41–44). The central honor in our Lord's life was His Father's honor; He "made Himself of no reputation" (Philippians 2:7). Every kind of scandal it was possible for people to think of was heaped upon Him, and He never attempted to clear Himself; but let anyone show an attitude of dishonor toward His Father and instantly Jesus Christ was ablaze in zeal; and "as He is, so are we in this world" (1 John 4:17).

Jesus Christ changes the center of our self-love. Is my honor God's honor? Are they identically the same, as they were in Jesus Christ? Let these statements analyze us: we are scandalized at immorality, why? Is it because God's honor is at stake? or is it not rather because our social honor is upset and antagonized? As saints, we should smart and suffer keenly whenever we see pride and covetousness and self-realization because these are the things that go against the honor of God. "You do not have love of God in you," said Jesus Christ to the Pharisees, and He pointed out that it was therefore a moral impossibility for them to believe (John 5:42, 44). No one with a standard of honor other than Jesus Christ's can believe in Him. Jesus Christ exalts the standard of honor and puts it alongside God's throne.

The real underlying reason our Lord "groaned in the spirit" (John 11:33 KJV) was because Martha and her sister had accepted a scandal against His Father. As soon as death came

on the scene, they accepted an interpretation that went against
the goodness and the love of God. The only thing that roused
Jesus Christ was for His Father's honor to be brought into disrepute. In the temple, instead of seeing a meek and gentle Jesus,
we see a terrible Being with a whip of small cords in His hand,
driving out the moneychangers. Why could not He have driven
them out in a gentler way? Because passionate zeal, an enthusiasm and detestation of everything that dared to call His Father's
honor into disrepute, had eaten Him up; and exactly the same
characteristic is seen in the saints. You cannot rouse them on
the line of personal interest, or self-pity or of self-realization;
but when anything is contrary to Jesus Christ's honor instantly
you find your meek and gentle saint becomes a holy terror. The
phrase, "the wrath of the Lamb," is understandable along this
line. The obverse side of love is hate.

(b) Humility

"Therefore whoever humbles himself as this little child is
the greatest in the kingdom of heaven" (Matthew 18:4; see also
Philippians 2:1–4). These two passages are a wonderful revelation; they show that the true disposition of a saint in this order
of things is humility. When the disciples were discussing who
should be the greatest, Jesus took a little child in His arms and
said, "Unless you become like this, you will never see the kingdom of heaven." He did not put up a little child as an ideal; if
He had, He would have destroyed the whole principle of His
teaching. If humility were put up as an ideal it would serve only
to increase pride. *Humility* is not an ideal, it is the unconscious
result of the life being rightly related to God and centered in
Him. Our Lord is dealing with ambition, and had He put up a
little child as a standard, it would simply have altered the manifestation of ambition. What is a little child? We all know what
a child is until we are asked, and then we find we do not know.

We can mention his extra goodness or his extra badness, but none of this is the child himself. We know implicitly what a child is, and we know implicitly what Jesus Christ means, but as soon as we try to put it into words it escapes. A child works from an unconscious principle within, and if we are born again and are obeying the Holy Spirit, we shall unconsciously manifest humility all along the line. We shall easily be the servant of all people, not because it is our ideal, but because we cannot help it. One's eye is not consciously on one's service, but on one's Savior.

There is nothing more awful than conscious humility, it is the most satanic type of pride. To consciously serve is to be worse than the Pharisee who is eaten up with conceit. Jesus Christ presented humility as a description of what we shall be unconsciously when we have become rightly related to God and are rightly centered in Jesus Christ. Our humility among people can only be understood by those who are Christ-centered in the same way. This is portrayed over and over again in the New Testament. Peter says, "They think it strange that you do not run with them into the same flood of dissipation" (1 Peter 4:4), and our Lord says, "When they exclude you . . . for the Son of Man's sake. . . . Leap for joy" (Luke 6:22–23). The center of the life is altered, and the worldling is hopelessly at sea in trying to find out the center from which the Christian works. The analysis of a Christian from a worldly standpoint results at first not in attraction, but in ridicule. The apostle Paul said that what he preached was foolishness, unutterable stupidity to the Greeks, to those who seek after wisdom; and that is the attitude toward the saints in this dispensation. A saint arouses interest for a little while, when things go ill he arouses deep interest; but when things go well, the interest gradually changes into ridicule, and then into his being absolutely ignored, because he is centered in Someone the world does not see, that is, in God. As long as a Christian complies with the standards of this world, the world recognizes him; but when he works from the real standard, which is God, the world cannot understand him and consequently it either ignores or ridicules him. Jesus Christ and the Spirit of God in the Epistles point out this antagonism between the spirit of the world and the Spirit of God; it is a deeply rotted antagonism, and as Christians we have to realize that if we obey the Spirit of God, we are going to be detested and ridiculed and ignored by those whose center is self-realization.

Our attitude in this dispensation manifests itself in a humility that cannot sting us into action on our own account. That is the thing that maddens the prince of this world. When the prince of this world and his minions scandalize Jesus Christ and misrepresent Him, the weakest saint becomes a giant, he is ready to go to martyrdom anytime and anywhere all the world over for the Lord Jesus Christ. We hear it said that the spirit of martyrdom has died out; the spirit of martyrdom is here. If scandal should arise against Jesus Christ, there would be many today who would stand true to the honor of the Lord Jesus Christ where in the past there would have been but one.

What is self-seeking? I must have self-seeking, and if my self is truly centered, my seeking is God's honor. God's honor is at stake in my eyes, in my hands and feet; His honor is at stake wherever I take my body. My body is the temple of the Holy Spirit, therefore I have to see that it is the obedient slave of the disposition Jesus Christ has put in to stand for Him. The center of my self should be God and love for Him. This question often arises: "I believe I ought to love God, but how am I to do it? How am I to have this tremendous love toward God? I agree that I ought to love Him, but how can I?" Romans 5:5 is the solution: "The love of God has been poured out in our hearts by the Holy Spirit who was given to us." Have you received the Holy Spirit? If not, Luke 11:13 will help you: "If you then, being evil, know how to give good gifts to your children, how much more will your heavenly Father give the Holy Spirit to those who ask Him!" Also John 17:26: "That the love with which You loved Me may be in them, and I in them." Ask God to answer the prayer of Jesus Christ. There is no excuse for any of us not having the problem answered in our own lives. Our natural hearts do not love God; the Holy Spirit is the only Lover of God, and when He comes in, He will make our hearts the center of love for God, the center of personal, passionate, overwhelming devotion to Jesus Christ. (God and Jesus Christ are synonymous terms in practical experience.) When the Holy Spirit comes in and sin and self-interest are in the road, He will instantly detect them and clear them out as soon as we give our consent, until we become incandescent with the very love of God. "Keep yourselves in the love of God" (Jude 21). That does not mean keep on trying to love God, it means something infinitely more profound, that is, "Keep the windows of your souls open to the fact that God loves you"; then His love will continually flow through you to others.

There are two terms used in modern psychology which are of importance in this connection: *projective* and *ejective*. *Projective* means that I see in other people the qualities I want but am without. *Ejective* means that I attribute my qualities or my defects to other people. The ejective method is seen in the matter of judging; when somebody has trespassed against me, I instantly impute to him every mean motive of which I would have been guilty had I been in his circumstances. "Therefore you are inexcusable, O man, whoever you are who judge, for in whatever you judge another you condemn yourself" (Romans 2:1). In Matthew 6:15 Jesus Christ puts the forgiveness of our trespasses on the ground that we forgive those who trespass against us. If we take the ejective method, we do not forgive them, we simply attribute to others what we would be capable of in the way of meanness in similar circumstances. The statement, that we only see what we bring with us the power of seeing, is perfectly correct. If I see meanness and wrong and evil in others, let me take the self-judgment at once—that is what I would be guilty of if I were in their circumstances. The searching light of the Scriptures comes over and over again on this line, and we come to find that there is no room in a Christian for cynicism.

3. Self-Estimation

(a) Superiority

This is a reiteration of the same point, that is, that self must be centered in God. Is my self Christ-centered or self-centered? When I am in difficult circumstances, does the disposition in me make me say, "Why should this happen to me"? That disposition was never in the Lord Jesus Christ. Whenever His consciousness was revealed, it was His Father's honor that occupied Him, not His own honor. My self is a human edition for God to be glorified in. "Let this mind be in you which was also in Christ Jesus" (Philippians 2:5). Could anything be more practical or more profound than that command? The mind of Christ showed itself in His actions and in His speech, and our minds are shown in our speech and in our actions. What was it that Satan antagonized in Jesus Christ? God-realization. Satan wanted to alter that center: "Do God's work in Your own way; You are His Son, then work from that center." At the heart of each of our Lord's answers to Satan's temptations is this— "I have come down from heaven, not to do My own will, but the will of Him who sent Me" (John 6:38). Jesus Christ was tempted, and so shall we be tempted when we are rightly related to God. "I have this against you, that you have left your first love" (Revelation 2:4). All the rest becomes of no account. To get eccentric, off the center, is exactly what Satan wants. He does not tempt to immorality; the one thing he makes his business is to dethrone God's rule in the heart. The superiority of

Jesus Christ's Self was that He was God-centered. "He who does not gather with Me scatters abroad" (Matthew 12:30), said our Lord; and all morality, all goodness, all religion, and all spirituality that is not Christ-centered is drawing away from Jesus Christ all the time. All the teaching of Jesus weaves round the question of self. It is not "Oh, to be nothing, nothing!" but "Oh, to be something, something?" Aggressively and powerfully something, uncrushably something, something that stands next to God's throne, on the Rock; to be those in whom God can walk and talk and move and do what He likes with, because self is personally, passionately in love with God, not absorbed into God, but centered in God.

(b) Inferiority

Selfishness means that which gives me pleasure without considering Jesus Christ's interests. Talk about selfishness on its bad side, and you will have everyone's sympathy; but talk about selfishness from Jesus Christ's standpoint and you will arouse the interest of very few and the antipathy of a great many. Sympathy for my fellow human beings is quite likely to rouse antagonism to God. Unless my relationship to God is right, my sympathy for people will lead me astray and them also; but when I am right with God I can love my neighbor as God has loved me. How has God loved me? God has loved me to the end of all my sinfulness, the end of all my self-will, all my selfishness, all my stubbornness, all my pride, all my self-interest; now He says—"love one another as I have loved you" (John 15:12). I am to show to my fellow human beings the same love that God showed to me. That is Christianity in practical working order.

16

OURSELVES: I, ME, MINE

Ourselves and Conscience

1. **Conscience Before the Fall—Genesis 2:16–17; 3:2–3**
   (a) Consciousness of Self—Genesis 3:1–24
   (b) Consciousness of the World—Genesis 3:1–24
   (c) Consciousness of God—Genesis 3:1–24[1]
2. **Conscience After the Fall—John 3:19–21**
   (a) The Standard of the Natural Person—Romans 2:12–15
   (b) The Standard of the Nations—Pagan—Matthew 25:31–46
   (c) The Standard of the Naturally Pious—Acts 26:9; John 16:2
3. **Conscience in the Faithful—1 Corinthians 8:7, 12**
   (a) Conscience and Character in the Saint—Romans 9:1; John 17:22

---

1. These three are the several sides of man's personal life.

(b) Conscience and Conduct in the Saint—2 Corinthians
    1:12
(c) Conscience and Communion of the Saints—1 John 1:7;
    Ephesians 4:13; Hebrews 9:14[2]

onscience is the innate law in nature whereby man knows
he is known." From every standpoint, that is a safeguarded
definition of conscience.

If conscience were the voice of God, it would be the most
contradictory voice anyone ever heard. For instance, a Hindu
mother obeys her conscience when she treats her child cruelly,
and a Christian mother obeys her conscience when she sends her
child to Sunday school and brings it up generally "in the training and admonition of the Lord" (Ephesians 6:4). If conscience
were the voice of God, contrasts of this kind would never occur.
"Conscience attaches itself to that system of things which man
regards as highest," consequently conscience records differently in different people. The conscience of the Hindu mother
attaches itself to the highest she knows, that is, the Hindu religion; the conscience of the Christian mother attaches itself to
the highest she knows, that is, the revelation of God in the Lord
Jesus Christ.

Probably the best illustration of conscience is the human eye.
The eye records what it looks at, and conscience may be pictured
as the eye of the soul recording what it looks at, and, like the
eye, it will always record exactly what it is turned toward. We
are apt to lose what Ruskin called the "innocence of sight." The
majority of us know what we look at, and we try to tell ourselves
what our eyes see. An artist does not use his logical faculties, he

---

2. N.B.: The half truth and half error of such phrases as "Conscience is the
   voice of God" and "Conscience can be educated" will be dealt with.

records exactly from the innocence of sight. When art students are being trained to sketch from nature, you will find that in looking at a distant hill draped in blue mist, with little touches of white or color here and there, the beginner will sketch not what he sees, but what he knows those blotches indicate, that is, houses; while the artist gives you the presentation of what he sees, not of what he knows he sees. Something very similar happens with conscience. The recording power of conscience may be distorted or perverted, and conscience itself may be seared. "Some will depart from the faith . . . having their own conscience seared with a hot iron" (1 Timothy 4:1–2).

Then, again, if you throw a white light on trees, the eye records that the trees are green; if you throw a yellow light on the trees, the eye records that the trees are blue; if you throw a red light on trees, the eye records that the trees are brown. Your logical faculties will tell you all the time that the trees are green, but the point of the illustration is that the eye has no business other than to record what it looks at; and it is the same with conscience.

To go back to the illustration of the Hindu mother and the Christian mother. The conscience of the Hindu mother looks out on what her religion teaches her to be God and records accordingly, and reasoning on the records of her conscience, she behaves cruelly. The conscience of the Christian mother looks out on God as He is seen in the "white light" of Jesus Christ, and reasoning on what her conscience records, she behaves as a Christian mother should. So it can never be true to call conscience the voice of God. The difference in the records of conscience is accounted for by the varieties of traditional religions, and so forth. Whether a person is religious or not, conscience attaches itself to the highest he or she knows, and reasoning on that, the life is guided accordingly.

The phrase, "Conscience can be educated," is a truth that is half error. Strictly speaking, conscience cannot be educated. What is altered and educated is a person's reasoning. A person reasons not only on what his senses bring him, but on what the record of his conscience brings him. When you face a person with the white light of Jesus Christ (white is pure, true light, and embraces all shades of color), his conscience records exactly what he sees, his reason is startled and amazed, and his conscience condemns him from every standpoint.

1. Conscience Before the Fall

The words *consciousness* and *conscience* meant the same thing originally; they do not now. In Conscience before the Fall we take the three aspects of a human being's personal life, that is, Consciousness of Self, Consciousness of the World, and Consciousness of God. "And the LORD God commanded the man, saying, 'Of every tree of the garden you may freely eat; but of the tree of the knowledge of good and evil you shall not eat, for in the day that you eat of it you shall surely die'" (Genesis 2:16–17). And the woman said to the serpent, "We may eat the fruit of the trees of the garden; but of the fruit of the tree which is in the midst of the garden, God has said, 'You shall not eat it, nor shall you touch it, lest you die'"(Genesis 3:2–3). In these passages the three aspects are clear—consciousness of self, of the world, and of God. It is the consciousness of God which has been most conspicuously blurred by the Fall.

(a) Consciousness of Self

This takes us back to the general subject of Man. When the other creations were passed before Adam in procession "to see what he would call them . . . . But for Adam there was not found a helper comparable to him" (Genesis 2:19–20). The human being has no affinity with the animal; this instantly distinguishes human beings clearly and emphatically from the animal creation around it. There is no evidence that an animal is ever conscious of itself, but a human being is ostensibly self-conscious.

(b) Consciousness of the World

We mean by the *world* the thing that is not my self, and *continuum* that which continues to exist outside me. By realizing how we come into contact with that which is not ourselves we realize our barriers and limitations. For instance we can never understand the consciousness of an angel, or the consciousness of a dog, because both these creations are constituted differently from the way in which we are constituted.

How do we come in contact with what is not ourselves? By means of a nervous system; consequently we can always say, up to a certain point, how another human being sees things outside himself. How do angels come in contact with that which is not angelic? Certainly not by a nervous system; therefore we have no possibility of knowing how an angel comes in contact with what is not angelic. Read the records in the Bible of angelic appearances, and of the appearances of our Lord after His resurrection; physical barriers simply did not exist to Him or to them. Physical barriers exist to us because of our nervous system. Angels can come and go through rocks and doors, can appear and disappear in a way we cannot understand. Their consciousness is above ours, different from it. When anyone tries to explain to you how an angel sees and knows things, say to yourself, "Private speculation." You will always find that God's Book puts the barrier clearly, thus far and no farther. Jesus Christ did not take on Him the consciousness of an angel; He came down to where humanity was, into the world we live in, and He took on Him a body and a nervous system like our own. Jesus Christ saw the world as we see it, and He came in contact with it as we do. (See Hebrews 2:16–18.)

We are only conscious of ourselves and of what is outside us by means of a nervous system; our conscious life depends altogether on our nerves. When we are asleep we are not conscious at all. What happens when we sleep? The world "goes out"; the nervous system is not working. An anesthetic makes the world "go out." The reason we shut up a lunatic in an asylum is because his nervous system relates him to the world differently from the majority of people. He does not record what he sees outside as we do, consequently he becomes so different and possibly dangerous that he has to be confined.

Now think of the lower animals. A great deal is said about the intelligence of dogs, and a great amount of talk about insight, falsely so called, into the nature of a dog. A dog is the most human of all animals, but yet we have no means of knowing how a dog sees what is not itself. We have no more means of knowing how a dog sees than we have of knowing how an angel sees; we simply take our own consciousness and transfer it to the dog. The recognition of these barriers above us and below us is essential to knowledge, and keeps us aware of our limitations. Spiritualists deny that there are any barriers; they claim that we can come in contact with angels, and understand how angels see things.

Remember, the body of a person is his glory, not his drawback. It is through the body that human character is made and manifested. The body is essential to the order of creation to which we belong; "Your body is the temple of the Holy Spirit" (1 Corinthians 6:19), says Paul, and we are held responsible for the way we manifest this fact to the world. When a person experiences a great alteration inwardly, his nervous system is altered. This explains what Paul says in 2 Corinthians 5:17: "If anyone is in Christ, he is a new creation; the old things have passed away; behold, all things have become new." Wherever the grace of God works effectually in a person's inner nature, his nervous system is altered and the external world begins to take on a new guise. Why? Because he has a new disposition. "If anyone is in Christ," his nervous system will prove that he is a "new creation," and he will begin to see things differently.

> Heaven above is brighter blue,
> Earth around is sweeter green,
> Something lives in every hue
> Christless eyes have never seen;
> Birds with gladder songs o'erflow,
> Flowers with deeper beauties shine,
> Since I know, as now I know,
> I am His and He is mine.

That is not only poetry, it is a fact.

(c) Consciousness of God

These three types of consciousness are clearly manifest in the way Eve talked to the serpent (see Genesis 3:2–3). Eve was conscious of herself, she was conscious of her surroundings, and conscious of God. In our Lord Jesus Christ these three aspects of consciousness were perfectly clear. With us, the consciousness of God has become obliterated, and we miscall all kinds of things "God." The system of things a person considers highest he is apt to call God. In Adam the consciousness of God was different from our natural consciousness; it was the same as in our Lord. Jesus Christ restores the three aspects of someone's personal life to their pristine vigor: we come into real, definite communion with God through Jesus Christ; we come to a right relationship with our fellow human beings and with the world outside, and we come to a right relationship with ourselves; we become God-centered instead of self-centered.

2. Conscience After the Fall

That is where we live today, that is, a mixture of Christian and non-Christian, and a great deal that is neither one nor the other. John 3:19–21 is the fundamental analysis: "Light is come into the world, and men loved the darkness rather than light, because their deeds were evil" (KJV). What is light? Jesus said, "I am *the* Light." He also said, "If therefore the light that is in you is darkness, how great is that darkness!" (Matthew 6:23). Darkness, in this connection, is my own point of view. When a person sees Jesus Christ and understands who He is, that instant he is criticized and self-condemned; there is no further excuse. Our Lord is the final Standard.

(a) The Standard of the Natural Person

The *natural person* means the one who has never seen or heard of Jesus Christ. In Romans 2:12–15 the contrast is drawn clearly and emphatically between what we may call religious and irreligious people. What is the standard of judgment? The Gentiles knew nothing about Jesus Christ or about the law of God as an external standard, and they were judged according to their consciences. Take the grossest case you can think of—nowhere is there any record of a cannibal tribe thinking it right to eat a human being; they always try to conceal it.

(b) The Standard of the Nations—Pagan

Nations are pagan nations, who likewise know nothing about Jesus Christ (Matthew 25:31–46). These verses are often applied to Christians, but their primary reference is to the judgment of the nations. The standard for Christians is not these verses in the twenty-fifth chapter of Matthew; the standard for Christians is our Lord Jesus Christ. In Matthew 25, God's magnanimous interpretation of the acts of certain people is revealed, and they are amazed and astounded—"When did we see You hungry? . . . when did we see You sick?" We never heard of You before. "Inasmuch as you did it to one of the least of these My brethren, you did it to Me." The standard of judgment for the natural person is conscience, and the standard of judgment for the nations is conscience.

(c) The Standard of the Naturally Pious

"Indeed, I myself thought," according to conscience, "I must do many things contrary to the name of Jesus of Nazareth" (Acts 26:9). If conscience is the voice of God, we have a nice problem to solve! Saul was the acme of conscientiousness. Our Lord refers to the same thing: "They will put you out of the synagogues; yes, the time is coming that whoever kills you will think he offers God service," they will think they serve God in putting you to death (John 16:2). That is the outcome of obedience to what is understood as conscience. No one who has read the life of the apostle Paul and his records of himself could accuse him of not being conscientious—he was hyperconscientious. *Conscience* is the standard by which men and women are to be judged until they are brought into contact with the Lord Jesus Christ. It is not sufficient for a Christian to live up to the light of his conscience; he must live in a sterner light, the light of the Lord Jesus Christ. Conscience will always record God when it has been faced by God.

3. Conscience in the Faithful

These verses show that we can be "spectacles" to other Christians. When the natural sight is faulty, spectacles are worn to correct the vision. We have to be as spectacles to others. So many Christians are shortsighted, so many are long-sighted, and so many have not the right kind of sight; be spectacles to them! A very humble position, but a very useful one.

In 1 Corinthians 7 Paul makes a distinction between equal

rights and equal duties. The Corinthians have been criticizing Paul, and from this chapter onward he is dealing with their questions, and evidently the whole point is the matter of equal rights. Paul says, "No! Equal duties, but not equal rights." We all have equal duties to perform toward God, but not equal rights. Paul deals with the matter in a statesmanlike manner.

There is a difference between "offense" and "stumbling." "So they were offended at Him. But Jesus said to them, 'A prophet is not without honor except in his own country'" (Matthew 13:57). "When Jesus knew in himself that his disciples murmured at it, he said to them, Doth this offend you?" (John 6:61 KJV; see also Matthew 5:29; 11:6; 13:41; 16:23; 17:27; 28:6–7). *Offense* means going contrary to someone's private opinion, and it is sometimes our moral duty to give offense. Did Jesus Christ know that He was offending the private opinion of the Pharisees when He allowed His disciples to pluck the ears of corn and eat them on the Sabbath day? Did He know that He was offending them when He healed the sick on the Sabbath Day? Certainly He did; and yet our Lord never put an occasion of stumbling in anyone's way. The passage which alludes to Him as "a stumbling stone and rock of offense" has another reference.

Stumbling, then, is different from offense. For example, someone who does not know God as well as you do, loves you and continually does what you do because he loves you, and as you watch him, you begin to discern that he is degenerating spiritually, and to your amazement you find it is because he is doing what you are doing. No offense is being given, but he is stumbling, distinctly stumbling. Paul works this out from every standpoint in 1 Corinthians 8 and 9. "As long as I live," he says, "I will never again do those things whereby my brother is made to stumble; I reserve the right to suffer the loss of all things rather than be a hindrance to the gospel: I will not insist on my rights, on my liberty of conscience, but only on my right to give up my rights." Waive aside your own liberty of conscience if it is going to be the means of causing someone to stumble. The application of this is what our Lord teaches in the Sermon on the Mount in practical experience. To put it crudely, the Sermon on the Mount simply means that if you are a disciple of Jesus Christ, you will always do more than your duty, you will always be doing something equivalent to going the second mile. People say, "What a fool you are! Why don't you insist on your rights?" Jesus Christ says, "If you are My disciple, you will insist only on your right to give up your rights."

God educates every one of us from the great general principles down to the scruples. People who are right with God are often guilty of the most ugly characteristics and you are astounded that they do not see it; but wait; if they go on with God, slowly and surely God's Spirit will educate them from the general principles to the particular items, until after a while they are as careful as can be down to the jots and tittles of their lives, thereby proving their sanctification in the growing manifestation of the new disposition God has given them. No wonder the Book of God counsels us to be patient with ourselves and with one another!

(a) Conscience and Character in the Saint

"I tell the truth in Christ, I am not lying, my conscience also bearing me witness in the Holy Spirit" (Romans 9:1; see also John 17:22). *Character* is the sum total of a person's actions. You cannot judge a person by the good things he does at times; you must take all the times together, and if in the greater number of times he does bad things, he is a bad character, in spite of the noble things he does intermittently. You cannot judge your character by the one time you spoke kindly to your grandmother if the majority of other times you spoke unkindly. The fact that people say of someone, "Oh, well, he does do good things occasionally," proves that he is a bad character; the very statement is a condemnation. *Character* in a saint means the disposition of Jesus Christ persistently manifested. You cannot appeal to a saint on the line of self-interest; you can only appeal to him or her on the line of the interests of Jesus Christ. The feeblest, weakest saint becomes a holy terror when Jesus Christ is scandalized. Whose honor are we seeking?

(b) Conscience and Conduct in the Saint

"For our boasting is this: the testimony of our conscience that we conducted ourselves in the world in simplicity and godly sincerity, not with fleshly wisdom but by the grace of God, and more abundantly toward you" (2 Corinthians 1:12). The point there is an important one; that is, that the knowledge of evil which came through the Fall gives someone a broad mind but paralyzes his action. The restoration of a person by our Lord gives him simplicity, and simplicity always shows itself in actions. Do not mistake simplicity for stupidity. By *simplicity* is meant the simplicity that was in Jesus Christ. Paul says, "I fear, lest somehow . . . your minds may be corrupted from the simplicity that is in Christ" (2 Corinthians 11:3). There are men and women of the world whose minds are poisoned by all kinds of evil, they are marvelously generous in regard to their notions of other people, but they can *do* nothing, every bit of their knowledge and broadmindedness paralyzes them. The essence of the gospel of God working through conscience and conduct is that it shows itself at once in action. God can make simple, guileless people out of cunning, crafty people; that is the marvel of the grace of God. It can take the strands of evil and twistedness out of a person's mind and imagination and make him simple toward God, so that his life becomes radiantly beautiful by the miracle of God's grace.

(c) Conscience and Communion of the Saint

"But if we walk in the light as He is in the light, we have fellowship with one another" (1 John 1:7; see also Ephesians 4:13; Hebrews 4:14). These references emphasize the "together" aspect. Nowhere is "Enthusiasm for Humanity" mentioned in the Bible; that is a modern phrase. Enthusiasm for the communion of saints is frequently mentioned, and the argument in these verses and many others is that if we keep our consciences open toward God as He is revealed in Jesus Christ, we shall find He will bring other souls into oneness with Himself through us.

First Corinthians 4:3–4 says, "But with me it is a very small thing that I should be judged of you or by a human court. In fact, I do not even judge myself. For I know nothing against myself, yet I am not justified by this; but He who judges me is the Lord." The apostle Paul mentions three standards of judgment which he has left behind:

1. Judgment according to the standard of the special class— "It is a very small thing that I should be judged of you."
2. The standard of universal human judgment—"or by a human court."
3. The standard of conscience—"In fact, I do not even judge myself."

The standard Paul accepts as the final one is our Lord—"But He who judges me is the Lord."

One of the greatest disciplines in spiritual life is the darkness that comes not on account of sin, but because the Spirit of God is leading you from walking in the light of your conscience to walking in the light of the Lord. Defenders of the faith are inclined to be bitter until they learn to walk in the light of the Lord. When you have learned to walk in the light of the Lord, bitterness and contention are impossible.

17

SPIRIT:
THE DOMAIN AND
DOMINION OF SPIRIT

Process of the Trinity

1. **An Instructive Parallel—1 Corinthians 2:1–14**
2. **What the Bible Says About the Godhead—John 4:24**
   (a) The Essential Nature of God the Father, God the Son, and God the Holy Spirit
   (b) Will—Exodus 3:14; John 10:17–18; 16:8–11
   (c) Love—1 John 4:8; Revelation 1:5; Romans 5:5
   (d) Light—1 John 1:5; John 8:12; John 16:13

   "The entire province of life, both in its lowest forms or stages and in its highest, is the province of spirit."

The Spirit is the first power we practically experience but the last power we come to understand. The working of the Spirit of God is much easier to experience than to try and understand, the reason being that we form our ideas out of things we have seen and handled and touched; but when we come to think about the Godhead and the Spirit, language is strained to its limit, and all we can do is to use pictures to try and convey our ideas. Yet in spite of the difficulty, it is very necessary that we should think as Christians as well as live as Christians. It is not sufficient to experience the reality of the Spirit of God within us and His wonderful work; we have to bring our brains into line with our experience so that we can think and understand along Christian lines. It is because so few do think along Christian lines that it is easy for wrong teaching and wrong thinking to come in, especially in connection with the Spirit.

1. An Instructive Parallel

For what man knows the things of a man except the spirit of the man which is in him? Even so no one knows the things of God except the Spirit of God. (1 Corinthians 2:11)

In these verses the apostle Paul is referring to the basis of how to think. The way we understand the things of anyone, he says, is by the spirit of that person; and the way we understand the things of God is by the Spirit of God; that just as the spirit of an individual knows the things of that individual, so the Spirit of God alone knows the things of God. This is the first principle that the apostle Paul lays down, and we must see that we grasp and clearly understand it. The next step is clear, that is, that we cannot expound the things of God unless we have the Spirit of God. There is an analogy, Paul says: as there is a law in the natural world whereby we reason and think and argue about natural things, so there is a law in the spiritual world; but the law which runs through the natural world is not the same as in the spiritual world. We can only discern the spiritual world by the Spirit of God, not by our human spirits; and if we have not received the Spirit of God we shall never discern spiritual things or understand them; we shall move continually in a dark world, and come slowly to the conclusion that the New Testament language is very exaggerated. But when we have received the Spirit of God, we begin to "know the things that have been freely given to us by God" (v. 12), and to compare "spiritual things with spiritual," "not in words which man's wisdom teaches but which the Holy Spirit teaches" (v. 13).

The apostle Paul here is at the very heart of things—as he always is, because he is not only inspired by the Spirit of God in the way inspiration is generally understood, but he is "moved by the Holy Spirit" in a special manner to expound the basis of Christian doctrine.

The things of God cannot be expounded by the spirit of any human being, but only by the Spirit of God. "But the natural man does not receive the things of the Spirit of God, for they are foolishness to him; neither can he know them, because they are spiritually discerned" (v. 14). For example, take the attitude of the "master in Israel" to Jesus Christ. Nicodemus believed that the germ of life was in him and in all people like him; but our Lord brought before him this truth which Paul is expounding, that is, "That which is born of the flesh is flesh, and that which is born of the Spirit is spirit. Do not marvel that I said to you, 'You must be born again'" (John 3:6–7).

Let us get this fundamental distinction clearly in our minds: we cannot penetrate the things of God and understand them by human intelligence; the only way we can understand the things of God is by the Spirit of God. Every Christian unquestionably is mentally agnostic; that is, all we know about God we have accepted by revelation, we did not find it out for ourselves. We did not worry it out by thinking. Or work it out by reasoning. We did not say, "Because so and so is true in the natural world, therefore it must be true in the spiritual world." We cannot find out God in that way. Jesus said, "If you would know My doctrine," meaning, My logic, My reasoning and My thinking, "first do My will, believe in Me, commit yourself to Me, obey Me; then you will know whether My doctrine is of God, or whether I speak of Myself" (see John 7:17).

There is a great deal of teaching abroad today which says that we have the Spirit of God in us and all that is needed is for it to be developed; if people are placed into the right conditions, the spirit in them will develop and grow and in that way they will come to understand God. This is contrary to all that Jesus Christ taught, and contrary to the New Testament all through. We have to come to the stage of realizing that we are paupers in our own spirits; we have no power to grasp God, we cannot begin to understand Him. If ever we are going to understand God, we must receive His Spirit, then He will begin to expound to us the things of God. We understand the things of the world by our natural intelligence, and we understand the things of God by "the spirit who is from God."

2. What the Bible Says About the Godhead

"God is Spirit; and those who worship Him must worship in spirit and in truth" (John 4:24). Jesus Christ is not implying that I must worship God sincerely; "in spirit" does not refer to my spirit, to human sincerity, but to the Spirit of God. I must have the same Spirit in me before I can worship God.

"God is Spirit." What is spirit? Instantly we find insuperable barriers to thought. Did you ever try for one minute to think of God? We cannot think of a Being who had no beginning and who has no end; consequently people without the Spirit of God make gods out of ideas of their own. It is a great moment in our lives when we realize we must be agnostic about God, that we cannot get hold of Him. Then comes the revelation that Jesus Christ will give to us the Holy Spirit, who will lift us into a new domain and enable us to understand all that He reveals, and to live the life God wants us to live.

(a) The Essential Nature of God the Father, God the Son, and God the Holy Spirit

The first thing to notice is that what is true of God the Father is true also of God the Son and of God the Holy Spirit, because they are one. The main characteristics which are the same in the Father and in the Son and in the Holy Spirit are Will, Love, and Light. The point to emphasize is that the essential nature of one person of the Trinity is the essential nature of the other persons of the Trinity. If we understand God the Holy Spirit, we shall understand God the Son and God the Father (see Matthew 11:27); therefore the first thing for us to do is to receive the Holy Spirit (Luke 11:13).

The essential nature of God the Father is Spirit. In order to show the difficulty of putting this into words, ask yourself how much room does thinking take up? Why, no room at all because thought is of the nature of spirit. It is by means of our spirits that we understand the things with which we come in contact. "God is Spirit" (John 4:24), therefore if we are going to understand God, we must have the Spirit of God. The human spirit takes up no room and the Spirit of God takes up no room, they work and interwork. My spirit has no power in itself to lay hold of God; but when the Spirit of God comes in to my spirit, He energizes my spirit, then the rest depends upon me. If I do not obey the Spirit of God and bring into the light the wrong things He reveals and let Him deal with them, I shall grieve Him, and may grieve Him away.

(b) Will

God said to Moses, "I AM WHO I AM." Then He said, "Thus you shall say to the children of Israel, 'I AM has sent me to you'" (Exodus 3:14). The first fundamental characteristic of God the Father, or God Almighty, is that of *pure free will*. There is no such thing as pure free will in any human; God Almighty is the only Being who has the power of pure free will. By His will He created what His breath sustains. The Bible revelation is that the essential nature of God is this power of free will.

What is the characteristic of God the Son? "I lay down My life that I might take it again. No one takes it from Me, but I lay it down of Myself. I have power to lay it down, and I have power to take it again. This command I have received from My Father" (John 10:17–18). No one has the power to lay down his life in the way Jesus Christ is referring to. Remember, Jesus Christ is God Incarnate, and the fundamental characteristic of God the Father is the fundamental characteristic of God the Son. Our Lord says, in effect, "I lay down My life because I choose to lay it down, and I take it again because I choose to."

"And when He has come, He will convict the world of sin, and of righteousness and of judgment" (John 16:8). The subject of human free will is nearly always either overstated or understated. There is a predetermination in the human spirit which makes a person will along certain lines; but no one has the power to make an act of pure free will. When the Spirit of God comes into someone, He brings His own generating will power and causes him to will with God, and we have the amazing revelation that the saint's free choices are the predeterminations of God. That is a most wonderful thing in Christian psychology, that a saint chooses exactly what God predetermined he should choose. If you have never received the Spirit of God this will be one of the things which is foolishness to you: but if you have received the Spirit and are obeying Him, you find He brings your spirit into complete harmony with God and the sound of your goings and the sound of God's goings are one and the same.

New Theology, Christian Science, and Theosophy all teach that God created the Being called His Son in order to realize Himself. They say, in fact, that the term "Son of God" means not only our Lord Jesus Christ, but the whole creation of humanity. God is All, and the creation of humanity was in order to help God to realize Himself. The practical outcome of this line of thinking is to make people say, "It is absurd to talk about sin and the fall; sin is merely a defect, and to talk about the need of an atonement is nonsense." The Bible nowhere says that God created the world in order to realize Himself. The Bible reveals that God was absolutely self-sufficient, and that the manifestation of the Son of God was for another purpose altogether, that is, for the solution of the gigantic problem caused by sin. The marvel of the creation of the human being is that he is made "of the earth, earthy." God allowed the Enemy to work on this human creation in a way he cannot work on any other creation, but ultimately God is going to overthrow the rule of His enemy by a being a little lower than the angels, that is, human. When God came into this order of things, He did not come as an angel, He came as a Man, He took upon Him our human nature. This is the marvel of the Incarnation.

We know nothing about God the Father except as Jesus Christ has revealed Him. "Philip said to Him, 'Lord show us the Father. . . .' Jesus said to him, 'Have I been with you so long, and yet you have not known Me, Philip? He who has seen Me has seen the Father'" (John 14:8–9). The characteristics of God Almighty are mirrored for us in Jesus Christ; therefore if we want to know what God is like, we must study Jesus Christ.

The first fundamental characteristic of the mighty nature of God is will; consequently when God's Spirit comes into our spirits, we can will to do what God wants us to do. "For it is God who works in you both to will and to do for His good pleasure" (Philippians 2:13). Will is not a faculty. We talk of a person having a weak will, or a strong will; that is misleading. *Will* means the whole nature active, and when we are energized by the Spirit of God, we are enabled to do what we could not do before; that is, we are able to obey God.

(c) Love

The next great fundamental characteristic of God the Father is Love. "God is love" (1 John 4:8). The Bible does not say that God is loving, but that God is love. The phrase "the lovingkindness of God" is frequently used, but when the nature of God is revealed, the Bible does not say God is a loving Being, it says, "God is love."

The same characteristic is revealed in God the Son, that is, love, and instantly the kind of love is shown: "Who loved us and washed us from our sins in His own blood" (Revelation 1:5), not a love that overlooks sin, but a love the essential nature of which is that it delivers from sin.

"The love of God has been poured out in our hearts by the Holy Spirit who was given to us" (Romans 5:5). This does not mean that when we receive the Holy Spirit He enables us to have the capacity for loving God, but that He pours out in our hearts *the love of God*, a much more fundamental and marvelous thing. It is pathetic the number of people who are piously trying to make their poor human hearts love God! The Holy Spirit pours out in my heart, not the power to love God, but the very nature of God; and the nature of God coming into me makes me part of God's consciousness, not God part of my consciousness. I am unconscious of God because I have been taken up into His consciousness. Paul puts it in Galatians 2:20 (a verse with which we are perfectly familiar, but which none of us will ever fathom, no matter how long we live, or how much we experience of God's grace): "I am crucified with Christ: nevertheless I live; yet not I, but Christ liveth in me: and the life which I now live in the flesh I live by the faith of the Son of God, who loved me and gave Himself for me" (KJV). Again in Galatians 1:15–16, Paul refers to the receiving of the very nature of Jesus Christ: "When it pleased God, who separated me from my mother's womb and called me through His grace, to reveal His Son in me." This is the true idea of a saint. A saint is not someone who is trying to be good, trying by effort and prayer and longing and obedience to attain as many saintly characteristics as possible; a *saint* is a being who has been re-created. "If anyone is in Christ, he is a new creation" (2 Corinthians 5:17).

We have to be solemnly careful that we do not travesty and belittle the work of God and the atonement of the Lord Jesus Christ. If we belittle it in the tiniest degree, although we may do it in ignorance, we shall surely suffer. The first thing which will make us belittle the atonement is getting out of sympathy with God into sympathy with people, because when we do this we begin to drag down the tremendous revelation that the essential nature of God is Will and Love and Light, and that it is these characteristics which are imparted to us by the Holy Spirit. We have not these characteristics naturally. By nature our hearts are darkened away from God; we have no power to generate will within ourselves; we have no power to love God when we like, and our hearts are darkened.

(d) Light

Again, the essential nature of God the Father is Light. "This is the message which we have heard from Him and declare to you, that God is light and in Him is no darkness at all" (1 John 1:5). There is no variation in God, no "shadow that is cast by turning" (James 1:17). We are told that where there is light and substance, there must be shadow; but there is no shadow in God, none whatsoever.

What does Jesus Christ say of Himself? "I am the light of the world" (John 8:12), no shadow in Jesus Christ. And of the Holy Spirit, Jesus said, "However, when He, the Spirit of truth, has come, He will guide you into all truth; for He shall not speak on His own authority, but whatever He hears He will speak; and He will tell you things to come" (John 16:13).

Active Will, pervading Love showing itself as Light in God the Father; active Will, pervading Love showing itself as Light in the Lord Jesus Christ; all-pervading energy and will and all-pervading Love showing itself as Light in the Holy Spirit. These are the fundamental characteristics of the Godhead.

To review: "God is love." No one who is wide-awake naturally ever believes that unless he has received the Spirit of God, it is foolishness to him. In the Sermon on the Mount Jesus Christ says, in effect, that when as His disciples we have been initiated into the kind of life He lives, we are based on the knowledge that God is our heavenly Father and that He is love. Then there comes the wonderful working out of this knowledge in our lives, it is not that we *won't* worry, but that we have come to the place where we *cannot* worry, because the Holy Spirit has poured out the love of God in our hearts, and we find that we can never think of anything our heavenly Father will forget. Although great clouds and perplexities may come, as they did in the case of Job, and of the apostle Paul, and in the case of every saint, yet they never touch the secret place of the Most High. "Therefore we will not fear, though the earth be removed, and though the mountains be carried into the midst of the sea" (Psalm 46:2). The Spirit of God has so centered us in God and everything is so rightly adjusted that we do not fear.

We cannot give ourselves the Holy Spirit; the Holy Spirit is God Almighty's gift if we will simply become poor enough to ask for Him. "If you then, being evil, know how to give good gifts to your children, how much more will your heavenly Father give the Holy Spirit to those who ask Him!" (Luke 11:13). But when the Holy Spirit has come in, there is something we can do and God cannot do, we can obey Him. If we do not obey Him, we shall grieve Him. "And do not grieve the Holy Spirit of God" (Ephesians 4:30). Over and over again we need to be reminded of Paul's counsel. "Work out your own salvation with fear and trembling; for it is God who works in you both to will and to do for His good pleasure." Thank God, it is gloriously and majestically true that the Holy Spirit can work in us the very nature of Jesus Christ if we will obey Him, until in and through our mortal flesh may be manifested works which will make people glorify our Father in heaven, and know that we have been with Jesus.

Light is the most marvelous description of clear, beautiful moral character from God's standpoint. "If we walk in the light as He is in the light, we have fellowship with one another, and the blood of Jesus Christ His Son cleanses us from all sin" (1 John 1:7).

"If we walk in the light."
What light?
"As He is in the light."
What light?
"I am the Light of the world."
What light?
The light of the Holy Spirit!

"This is the condemnation, that the light has come into the world, and men loved darkness rather than light, because their deeds were evil" (John 3:19). *Darkness* is my own point of view, my prejudices and preconceived determinations; if the Spirit of God agrees with these, well and good; if not, I shall go my own way.

The weaning that goes on when a soul is being taken out of walking in the light of its own convictions into walking in the light of God is a time of peril. When a child is being weaned, it is fractious, and when God is trying to wean us from our own ways of looking at things in order to bring us into the full light of the Holy Spirit, we are fractious too. If we persist in sticking to our own convictions, we shall end in darkness; but if we walk in the light, as God is in the light, recognizing and relying on the Holy Spirit, we shall be brought into a complete understanding of God's way and we shall have "fellowship with one another," with all those who are walking in the same light.

Then comes this wonderful thing—we shall have a purity of life in God's sight that is too pure for us to begin to understand; "and the blood of Jesus Christ His Son cleanses us from all sin" (1 John 1:7). Anything less than that—I say it measuring every word—anything less than that would be blasphemous. If God cannot cleanse us from all sin and make us "holy and without blame" in His sight, then Jesus Christ has totally misled us, and the atonement is not what it claims to be. Oh, if we would only get into the way of bringing our limitations before God and telling Him He cannot do these things, we would begin to see the awful wickedness of unbelief, and why our Lord was so vigorous against it, and why the apostle John places fearfulness and unbelief at the head of all the most awful sins. (See Revelation 21:8.) When the Holy Spirit comes in, unbelief is turned out and energy of God is put into us, and we are enabled to will and to do His good pleasure. When the Holy Spirit comes in He pours out the love of God in our hearts, so that we are able to show others the same love that God has shown to us. When the Holy Spirit comes in He makes us as light, and our righteousness will exceed the righteousness of the most upright natural person because the supernatural has been made natural in us.

18

SPIRIT:
THE DOMAIN AND
DOMINION OF SPIRIT

Mundane Universe

Spirit as Physical Force

(a) The World of Matter—Psalm 33:6; 104:30; 2 Peter 3:5

(b) The World of Nature—Genesis 1:2; Job 26:13

(c) The World of Self—John 6:63; James 2:25; Ezekiel 1:20; Revelation 11:11

The student will find that we claim that the Bible gives the working explanation of all things. We found in the last chapter that the fundamental characteristics of the Godhead are Will, Love, and Light; that God is the only Being who can will pure will, and that when we receive the Holy Spirit He energizes our spirits so that we are able to do the will of God. The present day is the dispensation of the Holy Spirit. We are familiar with the phrase, but do we understand sufficiently who the Holy Spirit is? The Holy Spirit is identical with God the Father and with God the Son, and being a person, He must exercise an influence. The more pronounced a person, the more powerful is his influence; but we have to recognize that nowadays the majority of people do not know the Holy Spirit as a person, they know Him only as an influence.

Spirit as Physical Force

By the *mundane universe* is meant the terrestrial world in which we live, the earth and rocks and trees, and the people we come in contact with. When we dealt with the physical world, we found that everything leads us back to the Bible revelation, that is, that at the back of all is spirit force—not matter and material things, but spirit. What is this tremendous force? The Bible reveals that the force behind everything is the great Spirit of God. A great change has come over what is called material science, and scientists are coming back to the biblical point of view, that is, that at the back of everything is spirit; that the material world holds itself in existence by spirit. In early days when people tried to explain the material world, they said that it was made up of molecules; then they found that those molecules could be split up, and the split-up elements were called atoms; then they found that the atoms could be split up, and that the split-up atoms were made of neutrons, protons, and electrons; then they discovered that these particles themselves are like whole solar systems.

These facts are significant because they point out the absurdity of the cry that the Bible and modern science do not agree; how could they? If the Bible agreed with modern science, in about fifty years both would be out of date. All scientific findings have at one time been modern. *Science* is simply the attempt to explain what people know.

An important aside—do not belittle the Bible and say that it has only to do with salvation. The Bible is a universe of revelation facts which explains the world in which we live, and it is simply "giving a sop to Satan" to say, as some modern teachers do, that the Bible does not pretend to tell us how the world came into existence. The Bible claims to be the only exposition of how the world came into being and how it keeps going, and the only Book which tells us how we may understand the world.

(a) The World of Matter

"By the word of the LORD the heavens were made, and all the host of them by the breath of His mouth" (Psalm 33:6; see also Psalm 104:30; 2 Peter 3:5).

These passages simply express what is revealed all through the Bible, that is, that God created the world out of nothing. The Bible does not say God *emanated* the world. The exponents of the clever modern idea of emanation say that God evolved the world out of Himself. The Bible says that God created the world "by the breath of His mouth" (Psalm 33:6). Meditate for a moment on the word *creation*, and see what a supernatural word it is. No philosopher ever thought of it, no expounder of natural history ever imagined such a word. We can understand *evolution* and *emanation*, but we simply do not know what creation means. There is only one Being who knows, and that is God Himself, and the Bible says that God *created* the heavens and the earth.

What is the *world of matter*? For instance, I am looking at a book, I see it is bound in a red cover, it is flexible, and has black marks on it. I can account by my senses for the redness and the blackness and the flexibility, but the one thing I cannot describe is what it is that awakens those sensations. I see a clock, and I would probably describe it in the same way as you would—that it is hard and smooth, and brown and white; I can hear a sound, and see its face, and so on, all of which can be described as the result of my sensations, but what is it that makes me have those sensations? The way we see things depends on our nerves, but what the thing is in itself that makes us see things in a particular way we do not know; that is, we do not know what matter is. The Bible says the world of matter was created by God; the way we interpret it will depend on what spirit we have.

(b) The World of Nature

The world of nature (Genesis 1:2; Job 26:13) is the order in which material things appear to me. I explain the world outside me by thinking; then if I can explain the world outside me by my mind, there must have been a Mind that made it. That is logical, simple and clear; consequently atheism is what the Bible calls it, the belief of fools. "The fool has said in his heart, 'There is no God'" (Psalm 53:1). An atheist is one who says, "I can explain by my mind to a certain extent what things are like outside, but there is not mind behind that created them."

In the beginning God created things out of nothing; matter did not exist before God created it. It was God who created it, out of nothing, not out of Himself. "The earth was without form, and void; and darkness was on the face of the deep. And the Spirit of God was hovering over the face of the waters" (Genesis 1:2). This verse refers to the reconstruction of things out of chaos. As we pointed out in dealing with the subject of Man, in all probability there was a former order of things which was ruined by disobedience, thereby producing the chaos out of which God reconstructed the order of things that we know, and that we so differently interpret.

"By Him all things were created that are in heaven and that are on earth, visible and invisible, whether thrones or dominions or principalities or powers. All things were created through Him and for Him" (Colossians 1:16). We hear it said that if God created everything that was created, then He is responsible for the presence of sin. The Bible reveals all through that God has taken the responsibility for sin. What is the proof that He has? Calvary! God created everything that was created; God created the being who became Satan and He created the being who became the sinner. But sin is not a creation; sin is the outcome of a wrong relationship set up between two of God's creations. From the very beginning God holds Himself responsible for the possibility of sin (see Revelation 13:8). Nowhere does the Bible say that God holds people responsible for having the disposition of sin; but what God does hold people responsible for is refusing to let Him deliver them from that heredity the moment they see and understand that that is what Jesus Christ came to do. John 3:19 is the final word on condemnation, "And this is the condemnation, that light has come into the world, and men loved darkness rather than light, because their deeds were evil."

We have seen that God is responsible for the established order of nature; but there are conflicting views about the world of nature. If you read the book of Job carefully you will find there that the world of nature is a wild contradiction; you cannot explain it satisfactorily at all. If you start out and say that God is good, you will come across some facts which seem to prove He is not good. How is it that we come to different conclusions about the world: one person sees everything as bad as bad can be, while another individual sees everything as good as good can be? It all depends on the spirit within. There may be as many accounts of the world of nature as there are human beings. That is why the world of nature seems such a contradiction. The spirit within one accounts for the way one interprets what one sees outside; and if I have not the Spirit of God, I shall never interpret the world outside as God interprets it; I shall continually have to shut my eyes and deny certain facts. I shall do what the Christian Scientist does, deny that facts are facts.

Along this line we see the limitations of trying to dispute with someone who says there is no God, you cannot disprove it to him; but get him to receive the Holy Spirit and his logic will alter immediately. That is Paul's argument in 1 Corinthians 2—that the human spirit understands the things of the human being, but that the human spirit cannot understand the things of God. If I have not the Spirit of God, I shall never interpret the world of nature in the way God does; the Bible will be to me simply an Oriental tradition, a cunningly devised fable. If I am to understand the Bible, I must have the Spirit of God.

As Christians, we recognize that we must have the Spirit of God for practical living, but do we realize the need of the Spirit of God for thinking? Christian workers use dangerous weapons against what they take to be the enemies of Christianity (but in reality against our Lord Himself) simply because they are not renewed in the spirit of their minds; they won't think on God's line; they refuse to make their minds work. We have no business to be ignorant about the way God created the world, or to be unable to discern the arm of the Lord behind things. When the Holy Spirit has transformed our practical lives, He begins to stir up our minds, and the point is, will we bring our minds into harmony with the new way of living? Jesus Christ laid down a remarkable principle for practical living and for practical thinking, that is, He taught His disciples how to think by analogies, "I am the true Vine." Is the natural vine false? No, the natural vine is the shadow of the real. "My Father gives you the true Bread from heaven." Is the bread we eat false? No, it is the shadow of the real bread. "I am the Door," and so on.

If we have the Spirit of God within, we shall be able to interpret in the light of God what we see with our eyes and hear with our ears and understand with our minds. "The sun shall no longer be your light by day; nor for brightness shall the moon give light to you; but the LORD will be to you an everlasting light." (Isaiah 60:19). May this not mean that the ordinary days and nights bring before us facts which we cannot explain, but that when we receive the Spirit of God we get a line of explanation? For instance, we cannot explain life, yet it is a very commonplace fact that we are alive. We cannot explain love; we cannot explain death; we cannot explain sin; yet these are all everyday facts. The world of nature is a confusion; there is nothing clear about it; it is a confusing, wild chaos. When we receive the Spirit of God, He energizes our spirits not only for practical living but for practical thinking, and we begin to discern the arm of the Lord, that is, to see God's order in and through all the chaos.

"I thank You, Father, Lord of heaven and earth, that You have hidden these things from the wise and prudent and have revealed them to babes" (Matthew 11:25). Our Lord thanked His Father that He was the only medium the Father had for revealing Himself; and the invitation "Come to Me" is given to disciples, not to sinners. Watch your own if you have been born again of the Spirit of God, and you will understand the condition of mind Jesus Christ is alluding to—"all you who labor and are heavy laden"; trying to think out what cannot be thought out, and Jesus Christ's message to all such is, "Come to Me . . . and I will give you rest" (Matthew 11:28). "I am the Way" (John 14:6). "If My Spirit is imparted to you, you will begin to see things as I do." "Do not marvel that I said to you, 'You must be born again'" (John 3:7), born again for practical thinking as well as for practical living.

It is a strange thing the indiscriminate way we are taught to think as pagans and live as Christians. So much of our thinking explanations are pagan; people who are being trained to teach others are taught to think as pagans, and the consequence is what we are seeing. We have to bring our thinking into line with the living Spirit of God, to take laborious trouble to think, to mediate on these things (1 Timothy 4:15), "bringing every thought into captivity to the obedience of Christ" (2 Corinthians 10:5). Never allow your mind to run off on wild speculations; that is where danger begins, "I want to find out this and that." The sin of Eve begins whenever the mind is allowed to run off at a tangent on speculations. "Come to Me," says Jesus. "I am the Way," not only the way to be saved and sanctified and to live as a Christian, but the way to think as a Christian. "Nor does anyone know the Father except the Son, and the one to whom the Son wills to reveal Him" (Matthew 11:27), and Jesus will reveal the Father to anyone who will come to Him.

(c) The World of Self

"It is the Spirit who gives life; the flesh profits nothing. The words that I speak to you are spirit, and they are life" (John 6:63; see also James 2:26; Ezekiel 1:20; Revelation 11:11).

Can Jesus Christ speak to me today? Certainly He can, through the Holy Spirit; but if I take the words of Jesus without His Spirit, they are of no avail to me. I can conjure with them, I can do all kinds of things with them, but they are not spirit and life. When the Holy Spirit is in me, He will bring to my remembrance what Jesus has said and He will make His Words live. The Spirit within me enables me to assimilate the words of Jesus. The Holy Spirit exercises a remarkable power in that He will frequently take a text out of its Bible context and put it into the context of our lives. We have all had the experience of a verse coming to us right out of its Bible setting and becoming alive in the settings of our own lives, and that word becomes a precious, secret possession. See that you keep it a secret possession, don't cast your pearls before swine (Matthew 7:6)—those are the strong words of our Lord.

To use an ingenious symbol—we read that when Jesus was led away to be crucified, "they had come to a place called Golgotha, that is to say, Place of a Skull" (Matthew 27:33), and that is where Jesus Christ is always crucified; that is where He is put to shame today, in the heads of people who won't bring their thinking into line with the Spirit of God. If people are inspired by the Holy Spirit their words are built on the Word of God. Paul urges us to be renewed in the spirit of our mind; and the way we are renewed is not by impulses or impressions, but by being gripped by the Word of God. The habit of getting a word from God is right; don't give up till you get one. Never go on an impression, that will pass, there is nothing in it; there is nothing lasting until a word becomes living; when it does it is the Holy Spirit bringing back to your remembrance some word of Jesus Christ.

In this way we are able to discern the arm of the Lord, and the "world of self" becomes what Jesus Christ wants it to be, but if we are ruled by a spirit other than the Spirit of God, for example, the spirit of my right to myself, we shall explain the world of self according to that spirit. We shall never explain things as Jesus Christ explains them, we will begin to patronize Him; or if we do not dare to patronize Jesus Christ, we will patronize the apostle Paul. Anything to appear up-to-date, because the spirit that is in a person, no matter how cultured and moral and religious, or how favorable it may appear to people, if it is not indwelt by the Spirit of God, must be scattering away from Jesus Christ. "He who does not gather with Me scatters abroad."

"Wherever the spirit wanted to go, they went, because there the spirit went; and the wheels were lifted together with them, for the spirit of the living creatures was in the wheels" (Ezekiel

1:20). This is a picture of the ultimate working of everything in harmony with God by His Spirit. "When the cherubim went, the wheels went beside them; and when the cherubim lifted their wings to mount up from the earth, the same wheels also did not turn from beside them" (Ezekiel 10:16). The cherubim are an Old Testament figure of the mystical body of Christ. Moses was told to make two cherubim: "And you shall make two cherubim of gold; of hammered work you shall make them at the two ends of the mercy seat" (Exodus 25:18); and yet God had said, "You shall not make for yourself a carved image—any likeness of anything that is in heaven above, or that is in the earth beneath, or that is in the water under the earth" (Exodus 20:4). The cherubim are not like anything in heaven above or in the earth beneath, but like something which is now being made, that is, the mystical body of Christ. This is prefigured in Genesis; when Adam and Eve were driven out of the Garden of Eden there was placed "cherubim at the east of the garden of Eden, and a flaming sword which turned every way, to guard the way to the tree of life" (Genesis 3:24). The cherubim are the guardians into the holiest of all, and when the mystical body of Christ is complete, all the machinery of this earth will be moved and directed by the Spirit of God.

To be *saved* and *sanctified* means to be possessed by the Spirit, not only for living, but for thinking. If we will bring our thinking into captivity to the Holy Spirit, we form what is termed *nous*. *Nous* is a Greek word meaning responsible intelligence. Whenever we get to this point of responsible intelligence, we have come to a sure line of thinking. Until the *nous* is formed in natural life and in spiritual life, we get at things by intuition, by impulse, but there is no responsible intelligence. The writer to the Hebrews refers to this, "By this time you ought to be teachers, but you want baby food again: by this time you ought to be robust and mature, no longer either children or fools, but men and women able to distinguish between right and wrong, between good and bad, with a thoroughly informed, responsible intelligence" (see Hebrews 5:12–14). How many of us have allowed the Spirit of God to bring us there and enabled us to think along Jesus Christ's line? Or do we have to say when these subjects are referred to, "Oh, I leave those things for other people"? We have no business to talk like that, we ought to be at our best for God. We have not only to be good lovers of God, but good thinkers, and it is only along this line that we can "test the spirits, whether they are of God" (1 John 4:1).

How are we going to test the teaching that is abroad today? A man or a woman may have a real Christian experience, but if the mind is not informed and disciplined, the intelligence becomes a hotbed for heresy. Our thinking would be revolutionized if we would bring our imaginations into line with the Bible context, that is, the heart of God. The Bible not only explains God, it explains the world in which we live; it explains not only things that are right, but things that are wrong. If we start out with the idea that everything is going well and all is bright and happy, and then there is an earthquake, or someone is killed by lightning, or there are tremendous floods, or a shocking murder, or worse crime, the idea with which we started out will be flatly contradicted by the world outside, that is, by the facts we see and know. The Bible and the outside world agree, but both the Bible and the outside world are an absolute puzzle to us until we receive the Spirit of God. When we receive the Spirit of God, we are lifted into a totally new realm, and if we will bring our minds into harmony with what the Spirit of God reveals, begin to discipline ourselves, and bring every thought into captivity, we shall not only begin to discern God's order in the Bible, but our eyes will be opened and the secrets of the world will be understood and grasped. When we read the records of history we shall begin to discover the way in which God has been at work, and we shall discover when we look at our own lives, not a number of haphazard chances, but some preconceived idea of God's which we did not know being worked out. We shall begin to find to our amazement that our lives are answers to the prayers of the Holy Spirit, and that at the back of everything is the mind of God.

"But we have the mind of Christ" (1 Corinthians 2:16), says Paul. To have the mind of Christ means a great deal more than having the Spirit of Christ. To have the mind of Christ means to think as Jesus thought, and He always thought from one center, that is, God. "For I have not spoken on My own authority; but the Father who sent Me gave Me a command, what I should say, and what I should speak" (John 12:49). Where did our Lord get His words? From the Spirit that was in Him. The tongue in our Lord Jesus Christ got to its right place because He never spoke from the spirit of His right to Himself; and our tongues and our brains will only be in the right place when we learn to obey the Spirit of God in thinking. Thank God we are given a line of explanation for everything under heaven. When we receive the Holy Spirit and obey Him, we find that Jesus Christ does satisfy the last aching abyss of our minds as well as our hearts. The one word ringing out over our mental life is "Obey! Obey!" Those of you who know what obedience means in the moral realm, bring it into the intellectual realm. Are you bringing into captivity every thought to the obedience of Christ? Are you continually being renewed in the spirit of your mind? Is your thinking in absolute harmony with Jesus Christ's thinking?

The day we live in is a day of wild imaginations everywhere, unchecked imaginations in music, in literature, and, worst of all, in the interpretation of Scripture. People are going off on wild speculations, they get hold of one line and run clean off at a tangent and try to explain everything on that line, then they go off on another line; none of it is in accordance with the Spirit of God. There is no royal road for bringing our brains into harmony with the Spirit of God has put in our hearts; we do not get there all at once, but only by steady discipline.

19

SPIRIT: THE DOMAIN AND DOMINION OF SPIRIT

Man's Universe I[1]

"In whose hand is the life of every living thing, And the breath of all mankind." (Job 12:10)

1. **Spirit in the Natural Man**
   (a) Natural Nous
   (b) Bewildered Nous
   (c) Spiritual Nous
1. **Spirit as Soul-Making Power**
   (a) Particular Form—Genesis 2:7; 6:17
   (b) Personal Form—Numbers 16:22; 27:16; Zechariah 12:1; Isaiah 19:3; Psalm 2:10

---

1. N.B.: We deal here particularly with spirit in the natural man.

    (c) Physical Form—Job 32:8; Genesis 7:22; Habakkuk
        2:19; Revelation 13:15; Job 34:14–15

2. Spirit in the Flesh
    (a) Independent—1 Corinthians 2:12–14
    (b) Dependent—Psalm 32:2; 2 Corinthians 7:1; James 3:15
    (c) Death—Romans 7:18–23; 8:5–7; 1 Peter 3:19

1. Spirit in the Natural Man

First of all we will deal with "nous." As already stated, *nous* means responsible intelligence both in a natural person and a spiritual person. Jesus Christ is the expression of the responsible intelligence of God. He is *Logos*, the Word of God Incarnate. There is the same thing in a person, that is, there is spirit.

(a) Natural Nous

The moment responsible intelligence begins, the natural life differs; some people never seem to reach it at all, they live as children and die as children, or more as simpletons than children. They have impulses and imaginations and fancies, but they never come to a responsible intelligence. A child is not responsible, but the statements of persons of mature intelligence are responsible; consequently we are judged by our words. It is quite true that there are times when we have to say, "Answer my meaning, not my words," but those times are exceptional. The things we express, the statements we make, and the thoughts we form, are all stamped with responsibility.

There is a capacity in a person apart from the Spirit of God to know that there is a God. "For since the creation of the world His invisible attributes are clearly seen, being understood by the things that are made, even His eternal power and Godhead" (Romans 1:20). We are speaking of natural *nous* apart altogether from the work of grace. As soon as a person becomes responsibly intelligent, he comes to the conclusion that there must be responsible intelligence not less than his own behind everything there is, and God holds every individual responsible for knowing that. "He who comes to God must believe that He is" (Hebrews 11:6).

The ordinance of God is placed in the natural makeup of a person, and when someone becomes responsibly intelligent he is able to discern a great many things, things which he calls "justice" and "righteousness," and the apostle Paul states that the heathen are judged by conscience (see Romans 1:20–21). We are getting very near the point where conscience becomes the responsible power working in a person's life. When we dealt with conscience, we called it the "eye of the soul," which looks out toward God, and how it records depends entirely upon the light thrown upon God. *Nous*, or responsible intelligence, which is nearly the same as conscience, discerns the ordinance of God written in the human spirit; therefore to say that people are not responsible for doing wrong is untrue to experience and to revelation. The Bible says that a person knows by the way he is made that certain things are wrong, and as he obeys or disobeys the ordinance of God written in his spirit, he will be judged.

"By faith we understand that the worlds were framed by the word of God, so that the things which are seen were not made of things which are visible" (Hebrews 11:3). It is not a question of swallowing a revelation, but of understanding with responsible intelligence how the world was made. This is simply a fresh emphasis on what has been emphasized all through, that is, the responsibility of those of us who are Christians in experience for being Christians in responsible intelligence. If we can form responsible intelligence as natural people, we must form it also as spiritual people. The Bible does not only teach the way of salvation, but the way of spiritual sanity.

(b) Bewildered Nous

In 2 Corinthians 11:3 Paul is referring to the devil beguiling Eve through his subtlety, and so bewildering her that she could not understand God's will or obey it, and he says, "I fear, lest somehow . . . your minds may be corrupted from the simplicity that is in Christ"; and in writing to the Galatians he says, "Who has bewitched you that you should not obey the truth?" (Galatians 3:1). This confusion of the responsible intelligence takes place at the beginning of the Christian life and people are in danger of becoming legal. "I am afraid for you, lest I have labored for you in vain" (Galatians 4:11), says Paul—lest you become all wrong, because you are going back to the old legal notions and trying to make yourselves perfect in that way. It is along these lines that the subtlety of Satan bewitches away from God a life that was coming under His dominion. Our Lord alludes to the same thing when He says, "the desires for other things entering in choke the word" (Mark 4:19), that is, they bewilder you. No wonder the first law of a born-again soul is concentration. We hear a great deal about consecration, but not so much about concentration.

"He is a double-minded man, unstable in all his ways" (James 1:8). A double-minded person is a ditherer, that is the description of a bewildered soul, the responsible intelligence of the natural person pulling and the responsible intelligence of the Spirit of Christ also pulling, and he does not know which way to take. "Let not that man suppose that he will receive anything from the Lord" (James 1:7). A person must decide whether he will be identified with the death of the Lord Jesus Christ, which will mean the turning out not only of the "old man," but of the old responsible intelligence, the old bondage, the old legalism, the things which used to guide the life before, and the forming of a totally new mind. It works out in this way: in your practical life you come to a crisis where there are two distinct ways before you, one the way of ordinary, strong, moral, common sense and the other the way of waiting on God until the mind is formed which can understand His will. Any amount of backing will be given you for the first line, the backing of worldly people and of semi-Christian people, but you will feel the warning, the drawing back of the Spirit of God, and if you wait on God, study His Word, and watch Him at work in your circumstances, you will be brought to a decision along God's line, and your worldly backers and your semi-Christian backers will fall away from you with disgust and say, "It is absurd, you are getting fanatical."

"For to be carnally minded is death, but to be spiritually minded is life and peace" (Romans 8:6). We are familiar with the carnal mind in the moral aspect: its enmity against God, its wrong longings and seekings; but it takes a good deal of courage to face the fact that the mind of the natural person is wrong in its responsible thinking, that is, it will give verdicts against what Jesus Christ says; it will decide straightaway that His responsible intelligence is that of a madman, or the irresponsible intelligence of a mere dreamer. We are using the phrase "carnally minded" in this connection to mean what is called common sense, the mature responsible intelligence of an unregenerate human being, and over and over again we find how this clashes with the teaching of Jesus before it harmonizes with it. We are bridging now between the bewildered and the spiritual *nous*. When the Holy Spirit comes in it confuses a person's reasonable intelligence and turns his thinking upside down, and he gets thoroughly bewildered (See Matthew 10:34). We are not dealing with the carnal mind here in the deep moral sense, but with the responsible intelligence which sets itself against the spiritual understanding and refuses to be reconciled to it, in the same way that it may refuse to be reconciled to it morally; and until common sense becomes sanctified sense (not "sanctified common sense," which is not a biblical phrase, nor does it have a biblical meaning), and the responsible intelligence has been reformed by the Spirit of God, this antagonism will go on. When we begin to think along God's line, we come up with an amazing clash against certain things which we have accepted as being inalienable rights for everyone, because Jesus Christ's teaching works from another standpoint, and this clash brings confusion and bewilderment for a time, until we resolve to remove ourselves altogether from the old ways of looking at things and to look at everything from the standpoint of the mind of Christ. "If anyone is in Christ, he is a new creation" (2 Corinthians 5:17), not his spirit alone, but spirit, soul, and body, and slowly the new creation is seen all through.

(c) Spiritual Nous

"For 'who has known the mind of the LORD that he may instruct Him?' But we have the mind of Christ" (1 Corinthians 2:16). The great benediction of the grace of God is that those who seem to have no natural *nous* are enabled to construct *nous* in the spiritual realm by the Spirit of God, and use it properly in the temple of the Holy Spirit. To begin with, a child has no responsible intelligence, and the same is true in the spiritual domain. When we begin the spiritual life we have the Spirit of Christ but not the mind of Christ. To have "the mind of Christ" means much more than having His Spirit; it means to have the responsible understanding of Christ. When we are born again, we find every now and then that the Spirit of God within us is struggling to get us to understand as God understands, and we are very stupid in the way we mistake the things the Spirit of God is trying to teach us; but when, in entire sanctification, the Son of God is formed in us (see Galatians 4:19), we understand with a responsible intelligence even as Jesus Christ did; consequently we are held responsible for doing through our bodies all that we understand God wishes us to do. Jesus Christ spoke what He knew His Father wished Him to speak, and He spoke nothing else; we must do the same if we have the mind of Christ. Jesus Christ worked only those works which He knew were the exact expression of His Father, "My Father has been working until now, and I have been working" (John 5:17). We must do the same. To form a spiritual *nous* means not only that the Holy Spirit energizes our spirits but that we allow Him to work out in a responsible intelligence in us.

"And we know that the Son of God has come and has given us an understanding, that we may know Him who is true" (1 John 5:20). The word *understanding* does not mean anything necromantic; it means that we understand with a responsible intelligence that which comes from God; and God holds us responsible for not knowing it. It is not a question of any uncanny spiritual influence, or of a flashing spiritual intuition, but of having the *nous*, our responsible intelligence, so obedient to the Holy Spirit that we can understand what is of God and what is not. In this way we begin to form a responsible spiritual intelligence, and we must take care not to grieve the Spirit of God along these lines.

"'For this is the covenant that I will make . . .' says the LORD: 'I will put My laws in their mind, and write them on their hearts; and I will be their God, and they shall be My people'" (Hebrews 8:10). That embraces everything—a full, mature, understanding intelligence on the part of the people of God, not being at the mercy of spiritual impulses, driven about by every wind of doctrine, but becoming mature, vigorous minded people who not only understand what the will of God is, but who do it.

2. Spirit as Soul-Making Power

We are dealing here particularly with spirit in the natural individual. Remember, the whole meaning of the soul is to express the spirit, and the struggle of spirit is to get itself expressed in the soul. In the natural life when an immature mind is trying to express itself, there are tremendous struggles and all kinds of physical exertions and efforts. It has no responsible intelligence, no vocabulary; when a child gets into tempers, it is often an attempt to express itself. When a young life is trying to express itself, it experiences exquisite suffering; it runs to music, it runs to theaters, it runs to literature—anything to try and get the power to express what is there in longing; and if a life goes on too long on these lines, it will never form a responsible intelligence, but will become most impractical. The discipline of the machinery of life enables us to get the power to express what is in us. That is the value of language. There is a great difference in languages; for instance, take the language of the Bible and the language we use today. The words of the Bible express the inner soul; the words we use today are nearly all technical, borrowed from somewhere else, and our most modern words do not express the spirit at all, but cunningly cloak it over and give no expression.

This kind of phrase is often heard from a young person, "Oh, I don't understand myself"; or, "Nobody understands me!" Why, of course, they don't; but we are responsible for not having a responsible intelligence as to where we can be understood (see Psalm 139). The meaning of education is not to pack in something alien, but the drawing out of what is in for the purpose of expression. One of the greatest benefits when a young life is trying to express itself is to have something to work at with the hands, to model in wax, to paint, or to write, or to dig, anything that will give an opportunity of expression.

If it is true in the natural life that the mind goes through all this turmoil in trying to express itself, it is just as true in the spiritual life. When the Spirit of God comes into me the same kind of struggle goes on. The Spirit of God tries to get me out of the natural ruts into line with Him and to get me to obey Him so that He can express Himself through my responsible intelligence. These are the throes and the growing pains of a life after being born again, and they go on until the mind of Christ is formed, and the old carnal antagonism is no more. The value of a spiritual teacher is that he expresses for us what we have been trying to express for ourselves but could not. Whenever a person or a book expresses for us what we have been trying to express for ourselves, we feel unspeakably grateful, and in this way we learn how to express for ourselves. Tribulation will teach us how to express things, our circumstances will teach us, temptations of the devil will teach us, difficult things will teach us. All these things will develop the power of expression until we become responsible in expression of the Spirit of God as Jesus Christ was the responsible expression of the mind of God Almighty.

(a) Particular Form

"The LORD God formed man of the dust of the ground, and breathed into his nostrils the breath of life, and man became a living being" (Genesis 2:7; see 6:17). The particular forms of nature, rocks and trees, animals and people, are all the outcome of the breathing of the Spirit of God. There is a true law of correspondence between the things which we see and the mind that is behind them. When we have in us the mind behind the things we see, we begin to understand how these things manifest that mind, but if we have not that mind we shall never understand them.

(b) Personal Form

"Let the LORD, the God of the spirits of all flesh, set a man over the congregation" (Numbers 27:16; 16:22; Zechariah 12:1; Isaiah 19:3; Psalm 51:10). These passages make it clear that everyone has a distinct responsibility of his own, that is, he can express the spirit of the prince of this world in a responsibly intelligent way, or he can express the Spirit of God in a responsibly intelligent way. This is what we mean when we say a person shows "soul" in his writings or speaking, he shows "soul" in his prayers and in his manner of living; we mean that he has the power to express his spirit, the personal note comes out all the time. God is a Person, and He expresses the peculiar stamp of His Person in all that He creates. When we have the Spirit of God and are forming a responsible intelligence spiritually, we begin to think God's thoughts after Him and to see His meaning, not by our natural intelligence, but by the Spirit of God.

(c) Physical Form

"But there is a spirit in man, and the inspiration of the Almighty gives him understanding. Great men are not always wise, nor do the aged always understand justice" (Job 32:8–9; Genesis 7; Habakkuk 2:19; Revelation 13:15; Job 34:14–15).

Our physical life is meant to express all that is in the spirit. The soul struggles in travail of birth until the zone of expression in the body is reached. Paul is stating just this idea when he says, "My little children, for whom I labor in birth again until Christ is formed in you" (Galatians 4:19). To begin with we have not our own bodies, but probably a body which is very much like that of one of our grandmothers or grandfathers, but every few years the physical form alters, and it alters into the shape of the ruling spirit. We may find a beautifully molded face begin to take on a remarkably ugly moral expression as it grows older, or we may find an ugly face begin to take on a remarkably beautiful moral expression. Sooner or later, through the turmoil in the soul, the physical life must express the ruling spirit. One grows exactly like one's spirit. If that spirit is the spirit of the human, one shall grow further and further away from the image of God; but if one has the Spirit of God within, one shall grow more and more "into the same image from glory to glory" (2 Corinthians 3:18).

3. Spirit in the Flesh

(a) Independent

"For what man knows the things of a man except the spirit of the man which is in him? Even so no one knows the things of God except the Spirit of God" (1 Corinthians 2:11).

The expression of the spirit is independent of the flesh to begin with, consequently there is a divorce between the spirit in a born-again person and the expression of the spirit in the life. Beware of saying there is no difference in the external life of someone who is born again and one who is sanctified. It is untrue to revelation and to experience alike; there is a tremendous difference. The spirit in a born-again person does not express itself in the flesh in the same degree that it does when the point of sanctification has been reached, because the body has not yet learned obedience to God. In the beginning the Spirit of God works in independence of the flesh and conviction of sin is produced. When the Spirit of God comes into a soul there is darkness and difficulty because He produces discernment of the wrong disposition, and this discernment makes the spirit yearn and long after being made like God, and nothing and no one but God can comfort the soul that is born of the Spirit. The only hope for that life is concentration on and obedience to the Spirit of God.

(b) Dependent

"Blessed is the man to whom the LORD does not impute iniquity, and in whose spirit there is no deceit" (Psalm 32:2; 2 Corinthians 7:1; James 3:15).

When the Spirit of God comes into me, He does not express

Himself straightaway in my flesh; He works independently of my flesh, and I am conscious of the divorce. I gain slow, sure, steady victories, but I am conscious of the turmoil. The soul is the birthplace of the new spirit, and the soul struggles while the spirit tries to express itself through the body. If I do not obey the Spirit of God, my spirit will become enchained to my flesh and be absolutely dependent upon it, and the clamoring of the wrong mind through the avenues of the flesh will gradually crush and grieve the Spirit of God. "Therefore, having these promises, beloved, let us cleanse ourselves from all filthiness of the flesh and spirit, perfecting holiness in the fear of God" (2 Corinthians 7:1). The Spirit of God works independently in me to begin with, just as my natural spirit does, and if I do not obey the Spirit of God the insistence of the flesh, of the carnal mind, will gradually defile everything He has been trying to do. When we are being brought into harmony with the Spirit of God and are learning to form the mind of Christ, "the flesh lusts against the Spirit, and the Spirit against the flesh" (Galatians 5:17); nevertheless we can, slowly and surely and victoriously, claim the whole territory for the Spirit of God, until at entire sanctification, there is only one thing, the Spirit of God, who has enabled us to form the mind of Christ, and now we can begin to manifest that growth in grace that will express the life of Jesus in our mortal flesh.

(c) Death

"For I know that in me (that is, in my flesh) nothing good dwells; for to will is present with me, but how to perform what is good I do not find" (Romans 7:18; see also 8:5–7).

Romans 8:6, "To be carnally minded is death," is very direct, and puts an end to all the absurd squabbles as to what is spiritual death. To be given over to an ordinary responsible intelligence which has not been reformed by the Spirit of God, is death, and that intelligence in its manifestation will develop further and further away from God, until a man or woman can sink so low as to be perfectly happy without God. Psalm 73 describes this condition: "There are no pangs in their death. . . . They are not in trouble as other men. . . . Their eyes bulge with abundance; they have more than heart could wish." The extraordinary thing is that that kind of individual is the only person that worldly people call "alive"! When a person has the Spirit of God in him and is slowly manifesting the life of Christ in his life, the world says he is "half dead." "They think it strange that you do not run with them into the same flood of dissipation" (1 Peter 4:4). "If anyone is in Christ, he is a new creation; old things have passed away; behold all things have become new (2 Corinthians 5:17).

Where are we with regard to this responsible spiritual intelligence? How many of us, as Christians with a definite spiritual experience, realize that we have to be continually renewed in the spirit of our minds (Ephesians 4:23) so that we are able to discern what the will of God is—the thing which is good and acceptable and perfect? (Romans 12:2). All the childish clamors, the being driven from pillar to post by every wind of doctrine, must cease (Ephesians 4:14), and the mature, sensible, strong, stable life begin. Nothing can upset that life, neither death, nor life, nor things to come, nor height, nor depth, nor any other created thing (Romans 8:38–39). Every power such a life comes up against, whether it be a material power or a human or a diabolical power, will be but another occasion for the forming of a deeper and more intelligent grasp of the mind of God. The only way we develop intelligence in the natural world is by coming in contact with things that are irrational and unintelligent, and in the things of God we form the mind of Christ by subduing all to a spiritual understanding.

20

SPIRIT:
THE DOMAIN AND
DOMINION OF SPIRIT

Man's Universe II[1]

1. Spirit in Its Freedom from the Flesh—Extraordinary

(a) Ecstasy—Acts 10:10; 22:17; 2 Corinthians 12:2–4;
Revelation 4:2
Sometimes with the body—Acts 8:39; 2 Corinthians
12:2–4; 1 Thessalonians 4:17; Revelation 12:5; Matthew
4:1.

(b) Emancipation
(1) Death—Luke 16:25; 23:43; Hebrews 12:23
(2) Deliverance—Hebrews 4:12; Galatians 5:24;
Colossians 2:11; Romans 6:6; Galatians 6:8; John
3:8; 20:22

---

1. N.B.: We deal here particularly with spirit in the spiritual man.

2. **Spirit Operating in Sense**
3. **Spirit Operating Inwardly**
4. **Spirit Operating Morally**

> And so it is written "The first man Adam became a living being." The last Adam became a life-giving spirit. (1 Corinthians 15:45)

The contrast in 1 Corinthians 15:45 is not a contrast of moral worth, but of revelation. The phrase "the first man Adam became a living being" refers to the great fact of God's creation; the phrase "The last Adam became a life-giving spirit," refers to God's regenerating work in the soul. The human spirit does not have life in itself, the human being cannot will pure will, or love pure love. The Holy Spirit has life in Himself, and when He comes in He energizes our spirits and enables us "to will and to do for His good pleasure" (Philippians 2:13). *Adam* does not mean the "old man," but our human nature. Never confound the "old man" with *Adam*, they are not synonymous terms, and never confound the old man with the devil.

1. Spirit in Its Freedom from the Flesh—Extraordinary

We mean by *extraordinary*, away from the ordinary, not contrary to it or against it, but out of it. We have to bear in mind that there are facts revealed in God's Book which are not common to our experience, and a great moment is reached in the mental life when our minds are opened to the fact that there are states of experience, either for good or bad, about which the majority of us know nothing. It is easy to ridicule these experiences, but ridicule may be a sign of ignorance; it may simply mean—I know everything that everybody can experience, and if a someone says he has seen things I have not seen, then I take him to be a fool and laugh at him. It is I who am the fool. Paul uses this argument in 1 Corinthians 1; he says the preaching of the Cross is foolishness to those who seek after wisdom. Again, in connection with the testimony to sanctification people will tell you point blank that no one ever was sanctified, and if you say that you are sanctified, you are a liar, or you suffer from hallucinations. It is quite possible that many of us may have this attitude to the extraordinary experiences recorded in God's Book.

(a) Ecstasy

"Then he [Peter] became very hungry and wanted to eat; but while they made ready, he fell into a trance" (Acts 10:10). "Now it happened, when I returned to Jerusalem and was praying in the temple, that I was in a trance" (Acts 22:17). "Immediately I was in the Spirit; and behold, a throne was set in heaven, and One sat on the throne" (Revelation 4:2). "I know a man in Christ who fourteen years ago—whether in the body I do not know, or whether out of the body I do not know—God knows—such a one was caught up to the third heaven" (2 Corinthians 12:2).

Ecstasy is a word applied to states of mind marked by temporary mental aberration and altered consciousness, a state in which a person is taken out of his ordinary setting into an extraordinary state where he sees and hears things apart from the bodily organs. Remember, this power may be for good or bad. A necromancer can take one's personality right out of his bodily setting and put him into another setting where he sees and hears altogether apart from his body.

In these extraordinary conditions the body is sometimes taken with the spirit. "Now when they came up out of the water, the Spirit of the Lord caught Philip away, so that the eunuch saw him no more" (Acts 8:39). In this phase of ecstasy the body is taken with the soul by extraordinary transportation, by a supernatural "airplane," something absolutely unusual. First Thessalonians 4:17, "Then we who are alive and remain shall be caught up together with them in the clouds to meet the Lord in the air. And thus we shall always be with the Lord," refers to the instantaneous change of a material body into a glorified body (see Revelation 12:5; Matthew 4:1). After the resurrection our Lord appeared to His disciples during the forty days before He ascended; that is, He had power to materialize whenever He chose. "He said to them, 'Have you any food here?' And they gave Him a piece of a broiled fish and some honeycomb. And He took it and ate in their presence" (Luke 24:41–43). In the Millennium we shall have exactly the same power as saints; we are to "meet the Lord in the air." Is that conceivable to you? If it is, it certainly is not conceivable to me. I do not know how I am going to stay up in the air with the Lord; but that is no business of mine, all I know is that God's Book reveals that we shall do so. The marvelous power which the glorified resurrection body will have is pictured in the Lord Jesus Christ. He could materialize whenever He chose, He proved that He could, and He could disappear whenever He chose; and we shall do exactly the same. Just think of the time when our thinking will be in language as soon as we think it! If we have the idea that we are to be penned up for ever in a little physical temple, we are twisted away from the biblical revelation; just now in this order of things we are confined in this bodily temple for a particular reason, but at any second, in the "twinkling of an eye" (1 Corinthians 15:52), God can change this body into a glorified body.

All we are arguing for is the need to have an open mind about things we can know nothing of as yet. If when an experience is recorded, I say it is nonsense because I have never had it, I put myself in the place of the superior person, an attitude I have no business to take.

The state of ecstasy, something that lifts a person right out of his ordinary setting, and the transportation at times of body as well as spirit, then is revealed in the Bible. A miracle? Yes, but not more of a miracle than the fact that I am alive. Why should it be thought more of a miracle for God to transform me into the image of His Son than for me to be alive now? How is it that I am alive now? How is it that the material wood of this table and the fleshly material of my hand are different? If we can explain the one, we can explain the other; God who has made the one made the other. The point we are emphasizing is that we have to remember that at any moment God may turn a person's calculations upside down concerning what He will do and what He will not do. Scientists reached the conclusion long ago that they dare not produce their "experiential curve" into the inferential region beyond. They say, according to the record of common experience such and such is the case, and any isolated experience is put by itself. They do not say it cannot be, but that it does not come into their line of explanation. No true scientist says because the majority of human beings have never had a particular experience, therefore it is untrue.

All this is essential to the subject of personality. As long as we are flippant and stupid and shallow and think that we know ourselves, we shall never give ourselves over to Jesus Christ; but when we become conscious that we are infinitely more than we can fathom, and infinitely greater in possibility either for good or bad than we can know, we shall be only too glad to hand ourselves over to Him.

Mystery there must be, but the remarkable thing about the mysteries which the Bible reveals is that they never contradict human reason; they transcend it. The mysteries of other religions contradict human reason. The miracles which our Lord performed (a *miracle* simply means the public power of God) transcend human reason, but not one of them contradicts human reason. For example, our Lord turned water into wine, but the same thing is done every year all over the world in process of time: water is sucked up through the stem of the vine and turned into grapes. Why should it be considered more of a miracle when it is done suddenly by the same Being who does it gradually? When Jesus Christ raised a person from the dead, He simply did suddenly what we all believe implicitly He is going to do over time.

Have any of us a sealed mind about these facts in God's Book which we have never experienced? Do we try and apologize for them, try to make out, for instance, that Philip was not caught away suddenly by the Spirit; that the apostle Paul was not "caught up to the third heaven"; that Peter did not fall into a trance and see the things he did see? There is always the danger of doing this. Accept these revelations as facts, and you will find your understanding illuminated as to how marvelously things can happen when the great mighty God is at work.

(b) Emancipation
(1) Death

We are dealing here with the spirit in its freedom from the flesh. We mean by *flesh*, this body we are in, not the "mind of the flesh." It is possible for someone's spirit to exist apart altogether from someone's body.

"And Jesus said to him, 'Assuredly, I say to you, today you will be with Me in Paradise'" (Luke 23:43; see also Luke 16:25; Hebrews 12:23). These passages refer to the place where the body is not—the unseen. The Bible points out that the human spirit is immortal, whether or not the person is energized by the Spirit of God; that is, the spirit never sleeps. Instead of the spirit sleeping at what we call death, at the breaking away of spirit from the body, the spirit is ten thousandfold awake. With the majority of us our spirits are half-concealed while we are in this body. Remember, spirit and personality are synonymous, but as long as someone is in the body his personality is obscured. When he dies his spirit is no more obscured, it is absolutely awake; no limitations now, he is face-to-face with everything else that is of spirit. "Son, remember . . ." (Luke 16:25).

Soul and body depend upon each other, spirit does not, spirit is immortal. Soul is simply the spirit expressing itself in the body. When the body goes, the soul is gone, but the moment the body is brought back, soul is brought back, and spirit, soul, and body will again be together. Spirit has never died, can never die, in the sense in which the body dies; the spirit is immortal, either in immortal life or in immortal death. There is no such thing as annihilation taught in the Bible. The separation of spirit from body and soul is temporary. The resurrection is the resurrection of the body.

Our Lord never speaks of the resurrection of spirit—the spirit does not need resurrecting; He speaks of a resurrection body for glorification and a resurrection body for condemnation. "The hour is coming in which all who are in the graves will hear His voice and come forth—those who have done good, to the resurrection of life, and those who have done evil, to the resurrection of condemnation" (John 5:28–29). We know what the resurrection body for glorification will be like: it will be like "His glorious body"; but all we know about the resurrection of the bad is that Jesus Christ (who ought to know what He is talking about) says that there will be a resurrection to condemnation. The question of eternal punishment is a fearful one, but let no one say that Jesus Christ did not say anything about it, He did. He said it in language we cannot begin to understand and the least thing we can do is to be reverent with what we do not understand.

(2) Deliverance

"For the word of God is living and powerful, and sharper than any two-edged sword, piercing even to the division of soul and spirit, and of joints and marrow, and is a discerner of the thoughts and intents of the heart" (Hebrews 4:12).

Many teachers make spirit and soul one and the same; when the Word of God comes into my heart it instantly divides between the two, that is how the Spirit of God convicts of sin. "And those who are Christ's have crucified the flesh with its passions and desires" (Galatians 5:24). What is *flesh*? Paul is not talking to disembodied spirits, to a lot of corpses, he is talking to living men and women, so he certainly does not mean "mortal flesh"; he is referring to a disposition within that he calls "the flesh." When Paul speaks of the body, he speaks of it as "mortal flesh"; when he refers to the old disposition, he calls it "the flesh."

"In Him you were also circumcised with the circumcision made without hands, by putting off the body of the sins of the flesh, by the circumcision of Christ" (Colossians 2:11; see also Romans 6:6; Galatians 6:8; John 3:8). *Emancipation* means deliverance while I am in the flesh, not counteraction or suppression; it may begin in counteraction, but blessed be God, emancipation is possible here and now. According to the apostle Paul, and according to the whole of the teaching of the New Testament, we can be delivered from the old disposition— "knowing this, that our old man was crucified with Him." Crucifixion means death. The majority of testimonies contradict what the New Testament reveals. With whom are we going to side? "Let God be true, but every man a liar" (Romans 3:4).

Emancipation does not remove the possibility of disobedience; if it did, we would cease to be human beings. To make the removal of the wrong disposition mean that God removes our human natures is absurd. God does remove the wrong disposition, but He does not alter our human natures. We have the same bodies, the same eyes, the same imperfect brains and nervous systems, but Paul argues—you used to use this body as an obedient slave to the wrong disposition, now use it as an obedient slave to the new disposition. "For just as you presented your members as slaves of uncleanness, and of lawlessness leading to more lawlessness, so now present your members as slaves of righteousness for holiness" (Romans 6:19).

2. Spirit Operating in Sense

We have been dealing with the emancipation of spirit from slavery of sin, now we come to the Bible teaching that the spirit can operate through our senses, so that we can express in our lives that we are delivered: no reckoning or hoodwinking ourselves, no pretending we are emancipated when we are not, but the manifestation through every cell of our bodies that God has done what we testify with our mouths He has done.

"The children of Israel . . . did not heed Moses, because of anguish of spirit and cruel bondage" (Exodus 6:9). Their anguish of spirit had so distorted their senses that they could not listen. "A merry heart makes a cheerful countenance, but by sorrow of the heart the spirit is broken" (Proverbs 15:13). When a person is happy, he cannot pull a long face; he may try to, but it is the face of a clown; when he is happy inside he shows it on the outside. If you hear a Christian with a sad face saying, "Oh, I am so full of the joy of the Lord," well, you know it is not true. If I am full of the joy of the Lord, it will pour out of every cell of my body. "I had no rest in my spirit, because I did not find Titus my brother" (2 Corinthians 2:13). "While Paul waited for them at Athens, his spirit was provoked within him when he saw that the city was given over to idols" (Acts 17:16). "When Jesus, therefore, saw her weeping . . . He groaned in the spirit and troubled Himself" (John 11:33). All these passages refer to spirit showing itself instantly in the flesh. The spirit of wrong shows itself in the flesh, and, thank God, the Spirit of God does the same.

As soon as we become rightly related to God, the prince of this world has his last stake in the flesh; he will suck every bit of your physical life out of you if he can. Many Christian workers do not know this, and Satan will seek to wear them out to the last cell; but if they know this trick of his and also know God's grace, every time they are exhausted in work for God, they will get supernatural physical recuperation, and the proof that it is God's work is the experience of this supernatural recuperation. If you become exhausted in doing work in the world, what have you to do? You have to take an iron tonic and a vacation, but if you are exhausted in God's work, neither an iron tonic nor a vacation can touch you, the only thing that will recuperate you is God Himself. Paul said he did not count his life dear to himself so that he might finish his course with joy; and when the dear sisters and brothers say to you, "You must not work so hard," simply say, "Get behind me, Satan!" Remember, Satan's last stake is in the flesh, and when you know that all your fresh springs are in God, you will draw on Him. Beware of laying off before God tells you to; if you lay off before God tells you to, you will rust, and that leads to dry rot always.

3. Spirit Operating Inwardly

The spirit operates outwardly through our senses, and operates inwardly toward God. "In that hour Jesus rejoiced in the Spirit and said, 'I thank You, Father, Lord of heaven and earth, that You have hidden these things from the wise and prudent and revealed them to babes'" (Luke 10:21). Our Lord was talking to God inwardly by His Spirit. "These things we also speak, not in words which man's wisdom teaches but which the Holy Spirit teaches, comparing spiritual things with spiritual"

(1 Corinthians 2:13). If you have the Spirit of God in you, the preaching of the Cross is according to the wisdom of God: if you have not the Spirit of God in you, the preaching of Christ crucified is foolishness.

"For if I pray in a tongue, my spirit prays, but my understanding is unfruitful" (1 Corinthians 14:14–16). The question of tongues here is not a question of foreign languages, but what is called *glossalalia*, spiritual gibberish, nothing intelligible in it. Such phrases as "Hallelujah!" and "Glory be to God!" come about in this way. Just as a baby babbles for expression before its human spirit has worked through its soul, so a soul when being born of the Holy Spirit is apt to be carried away with emotional ecstasy. If you try to understand a baby's babbling, you cannot, unless you are its mother, then possibly you may.

In dealing with the Corinthians, Paul tells them to form a spiritual *nous*, an understanding whereby the spirit can be expressed. When a soul is first introduced to the heavenly domain by the Spirit of God, there is a tremendous bursting up of new life in the soul and there is no language for it. Paul urges the Corinthians to form a spiritual *nous* as soon as they can, to come to the point of understanding whereby the spirit can be expressed. "Therefore if the whole church comes together in one place, and all speak with tongues, and there come in those who are uninformed or unbelievers, will they not say that you are out of your mind?" (14:23). In the modern tongues movement the responsibility is with the teachers. May God have mercy on them!

When we are introduced by the Spirit of God into a new domain, we have no language; we are in a phase of spiritual babyhood; we have sighings and groanings and tears, but no language. Paul counsels us to be instructed, and one of the wisest ways of instruction is to let the psalms express for you. When you are worked up to a pitch emotionally, read some of the psalms, and the Spirit of God will gradually teach you how to form a spiritual *nous*, a mind whereby you will not only understand but will slowly and surely get to the place where you can express your spirit; you will have a totally new language. We read that "when the day of Pentecost was fully come . . . they were all filled with the Holy Spirit, and began to speak with other tongues, as the Spirit gave them utterance" (Acts 2:1–4). This was not glossalalia, it was the gift of new language.

4. Spirit Operating Morally

"Then everyone came whose heart was stirred, and everyone whose spirit was willing, and they brought the LORD's offering for the work of the tabernacle of meeting, for all its service, and for the holy garments" (Exodus 35:21; see also Proverbs 16:18; Isaiah 11:2; Acts 19:21; 20:22).

The Spirit, working through the senses and working inwardly to God, produces a morality and an uprightness just like Jesus Christ's. The worthiness of our Lord Jesus Christ is moral worth in the divine and in the human sphere, and our moral worth is to be of the same order.

God grant that we may ever "walk in the Spirit, and . . . not fulfill the lust of the flesh" (Galatians 5:16).

This book ends abruptly, but we leave it so. The whole book is merely a verbatim report of lectures given at the Bible Training College, and we have decided to let it go for what it is worth—a mere effort to rouse up the average Christian worker to study the wealth of the Scriptures, and thus become better equipped for rightly dividing the word of truth. God bless all who care to read the book!

NOTE TO THE READER

The publisher invites you to share your response to the message of this book by writing Discovery House Publishers, PO Box 3566, Grand Rapids, MI 49501, USA. For information about other Discovery House books, music, videos, or DVDs, contact us at the same address or call 1-800-653-8333. Find us on the Internet at http://www.dhp.org/ or send e-mail to books@dhp.org.